# Geeking Out

Using the Skills you Have and a Computer to Make Money

## Matthew J. Fitzgerald

## DISCLAIMER

The information presented in this book is advice only. It is not guaranteed to work for every idea and is provided as is without any warranty. Many factors determine the success or failure of business ventures.

The author and publisher are not responsible for your actions based on the information presented in this book.

The author and publisher do not promote 'get rich quick schemes' nor find any validity in their business practices.

# DEDICATION

This book is dedicated to Mom, Dad, and Katie, my family, friends, and all who have supported me through my many entrepreneurial ventures. They have provided their skills, time, and talents to ensure my success.

# CONTENTS

# ACKNOWLEDGMENTS

To Jim and Jeneen for raising me right
To Katie for putting up with me
To my friends for also putting up with me
To my professors at Purdue for teaching me about Entrepreneurship
and The Design Process

# INTRODUCTION

In my years of being an Entrepreneur, I have noticed that there is no good book out there that tries to help people create businesses specifically online. In our technologically changing world, nobody has started to bridge that gap between the more traditional business startup process by writing a book about this specific subject.

Everyone is unique. The skill and abilities we have can be used in a constructive way to build a business online.

The world changed once commercial internet services became available in the mid-1990s. No longer was it required to have a physical presence for getting some work done. Traditionally, in the event that you had a particular skill, you were required to look for a place that wanted to employ you. This metaphorical ball and chain tied to a company limited your creative and earning potential in any geographic area. With the advent of the internet, you can take your skill to multiple buyers across the world and build a theoretically limitless portfolio for yourself. The internet has truly created a world without boundaries; this is a diplomatic feat humankind has not accomplished yet, as history can tell us.

The internet has allowed people from all over the world the ability to work with other people who may not even be in the same country as you. I often have teleconferences with people in China or Egypt and have come to know the beautiful impact the internet has made on our lives. Through this boundless and seamless collaboration, the internet has fostered a global workforce that can work together to do great things and help the common good of society.

Today, the need for a middleman business to recognize your skill has diminished. You can directly approach the end buyer who is interested in your craft. Let me give you a simple example – In the brick and mortar world, a photo studio would employ a photographer and an image editor for taking a good picture and then cleaning and enhancing it for print and the photo's required applications. The photo studio had to recognize the talent of the photographer and the expertise of the image editor. Now in the new internet world, the two skill sets sell separately, and neither of the two must go to a photo studio for a job. The buyers are also not limited to the local geographical market in the sense of photo editing anymore, making life better for every skilled person.

This conundrum has created a new way of grabbing hold of the internet market. Today, not knowing how to market your freelance skills online puts you at a disadvantage in the global community. Not knowing how to position yourself and sell your services online sets you behind any individual with comparable skill and the knowledge of how to market themselves on the internet. This book endeavors to demystify the internet-based business model for you. Believe me, it is much simpler than it seems, and it is a bunch of fun as well!

Coming out of high school, I created Fitzgerald Tech Solutions to help people with a skill or an idea, but limited understanding of the marketing benefits of an internet presence show their product to the world.  Our goal is to help people benefit from the knowledge of the internet and the reach it provides for your business.

This book is part of my efforts towards putting a structure around ways of building your brand on the internet and making good money while doing so.

This book is my attempt at bringing structure to your commercial venture online. The book is divided into 15 chapters, each touching upon a critical area of building an online business and creating a scalable and successful business model. This guide is a compilation put together with our experience over the years, richly borrowing from models developed by others and the knowledgebase built while working with clients at Fitzgerald Tech Solutions and as corporate citizens.

Read through and let this get absorbed in your mind. If you wish, we can then work with you to build your unique business online.

Throughout this book, I will offer blank sections for you to be able to fill in the essential segments of a business model as well as help you ideate to make sure you find the business that is the perfect fit for you! I invite you to treat this like a workbook—write in it, scribble ideas in it, and use all of the forms to its max! If you are reading this book online, I invite you to get a notebook or scratch pad and copy the forms to a physical copy or electronic running document to fully develop a business plan!

Enjoy!

# 1 DETERMINING THE SKILLS YOU HAVE
The starting point – basics to help build a winning outlook

Before the advent of the internet, if you were a writer, the only way you could make a living was to get a job at a publication/advertising agency/publisher. You may have had to travel a long distance from home for that excellent job. Success would depend on reaching a few high and mighty publishers that were in a geographically reachable limit for you.

When the internet started to take hold in society at the dawn of the new century, people were merely beginning to discover the wonders of this brand-new tool. Major players in the eCommerce fields were just getting started: Jeff Bezos at Amazon, and Elon Musk at PayPal for example. As the internet has matured, we are seeing the creation of more and more global commerce happening online—and not in the traditional sense of the word.

The world is now very different. Your work can be sold across the world while you continue to be stationed in your home office.

Interacting with buyers is now easy. Many platforms are available to connect you with the buyers remotely.

Today, we see more of a transfer of services online that would usually have a home base located in a central office. People are now able to do what they would be able to do at the office at home, on the go, or halfway across the globe. The internet has changed the way we do business: We are now starting to develop a global, service-oriented economy online economy where people can make money using only the computer and the skills they have.

Figure 1: We are all different people!

Each person is unique. This uniqueness means we all have different personas and talents that allow us to stand above the rest. Imagine if every single person had the same skills, abilities, and lifestyle. The world would be an incredibly competitive place to live in.

Imagine for once, every single person in the world is a fantastic photographer. Trying to find a job would be difficult, there would be absolutely no demand for any photography services, and the world would be beautifully represented in portraits. Every person would be able to take beautiful family pictures for themselves, and they would look fantastic. What is the point of all of this if there is nobody able to consume the images or print them? Every single person shares this unique skill, but the things that set them apart are what they can do *beyond* merely taking the pictures. Printing them, editing them, and marketing them are some of the skills that would be incredibly helpful, valuable, and marketable in a world like this.

Throughout this book, being different is a significant factor in achieving a successful venture. Your clients want something different that sets you apart from everyone else. They want something that goes against the norm. This can help you carve your niche and discover what your business is all about and what your consumers want to see in the perfect fit for their needs. This can also help your customers learn how they can benefit from your service that accurately satisfies the products or services they are looking for.

Skills help us develop new products, ideas, and make better our way of life. It allows us to earn money and live the way we want to live. By being an entrepreneur, you are in control of your destiny. If you do not like something, change it!

Whether you realize it or not, by merely picking up this book, you are an entrepreneur.

*Figure 2: An entrepreneur requires many skills to be successful*

## What is an Entrepreneur?

According to Steve Tobak's article on the aptly named Entrepreneur.com website, "[An entrepreneur is] one who organizes, manages, and assumes the *risks* of a *business* or enterprise." While this definition is a rather matter of fact interpretation of what it means to be an entrepreneur, my definition varies slightly.

To me, an entrepreneur is an individual who has the drive, power, and determination to bring an idea from concept to a million-dollar company.

Some people think that being an entrepreneur is a onetime deal-- You try an idea, and if it fails, you are done. In reality, though, it is crucial not to let failure get you down. A well thought out and tested plan is bound to succeed! Throughout this book, I will be using the term entrepreneur a whole bunch and thought it would probably be a good idea to define what it truly means to be an entrepreneur.

One of the shortcomings of this introduction to the concept does not accurately represent all it means to be an entrepreneur. Being an entrepreneur is all about taking a calculated risk. Calculated risk is much different from your run of the mill normal risk. Normal risk is a complete shot in the dark where you are blindly throwing money at something without any form of external guidance and help. Think of putting on a blindfold and throwing money at a bonfire. It could go into the blaze and burn up, or it could land next to the fire and be saved.

Being an entrepreneur is different; you engage in taking calculated risks. By following the process outlined in this book and taking the time and effort in researching, developing, and testing your concept, you mitigate the risk of a business failing. This process is calculated risk. Taking the most effort before all of your money and time are on the line can save you from being put in a less desirable position in the long run.

A successful entrepreneur embraces the research, testing, and failure of ideas before they take the idea to market. In my own experiences, I have had ideas for products I have thought would be the next million-dollar idea, but through industry research, testing, and talking to people, I was able to determine that some of the ideas I had thought were great were not going to work in the market.

This concept relates to Steve Tobak's definition of the term, because being an entrepreneur involves a fair amount of risk to it, albeit calculated at that.

As for the rest of both definitions, I will flesh out later how being a successful entrepreneur allows you to manage and own an online business successfully.

## Types of Entrepreneurs

In my experience of working with different people and on various projects, I have developed my own categorization of what type of entrepreneur you can be. I have noticed that different entrepreneurs experience different traits and success levels based on their personalities. I will detail them below:

*Figure 3: A gap, or a missing piece!*

## The Gap Finder

This type of entrepreneur is the most successful of the three I will detail. They are the ones who look at an existing market, find the problems (gap) in the current offerings, and innovate based on that. These people are always curious and never satisfied with 'just all right.' They only want to be the best. Since this is the approach I take throughout the rest of the book and has been proven as the markets change and the economy grows, I will not detail it too much here.

*Figure 4: Creating a new market requires a groundbreaking idea*

## The Market Creator

These entrepreneurs are the visionaries: The people who want to make something unheard of before. They want to create a new industry and a new market for something people did not even know they wanted or needed. These entrepreneurs want to *own* their market. They want to be the go-to source in a specific area. In my experiences of working with people who want to create their own market, it is imperative to do a sufficient amount of research before taking any measures too drastic to mitigate the chance of failure. People who are this type of entrepreneur are incredibly driven and innovative. They *only* accept success.

*Figure 5: Fireworks are beautiful... while they last!*

## The Firework

This type of entrepreneur is a tad different from the rest. They are super pumped up for an idea and will go to great lengths to bring an idea to fruition for the first couple of months and then quickly lose interest, and then the idea gets shelved and dies a forgetful death. I like to compare this phenomenon to that of a firework. As the firework launches, there is so much hope and anticipation of what is to come. As the firework explodes, it is a beautiful sight—vivid colors, bright lights, and a KABOOM! Pounding your chest. Sadly, the firework is short-lived and quickly fades away into the night sky. The entrepreneur is like the firework, much promise, great results, but short-lived. Unfortunately, I have seen this more than I care to admit, and it truly is a shame. Many factors lead someone to shelve an idea, but being a successful entrepreneur requires dedication and commitment to an idea and a purpose.

By sharing what I consider the three types of entrepreneurs, hopefully, you can gain some guidance on some of the simple traits it takes to be successful. Later, I will discuss more in-depth about what characteristics I have identified in entrepreneurs who successfully run their startup.

# Getting Started

To start on this complicated thing called our online venture, we need to build a few basics around which our business idea can take shape. The core of the business idea is the skill that we want to market, the one we have the highest conviction around. This core skill is then peppered with a few unique ingredients – skills or values we must inculcate so that we can build a successful and rewarding business.

Everyone is unique, and this makes us our own Unique Special Product, or USP for short. The world appreciates diversity in many ways, and thus, buyers continually look for the new and the fresh, or to put it simply, the gig with a twist. The core skill you want to market may be in writing, singing, teaching, design, software, technology, or marketing, to name a few. You name it, and a buyer is waiting to pay for the skill somewhere on the internet—and that is the beauty of our incredibly interconnected and united digital world. Skills help us differentiate from any form of competition; it gives us individuality, which is highly priced in the market. Identifying what differentiates you gives you the edge that will help you achieve success in not only your online venture but your life as a whole as well. The market values what you can deliver that is apart from the norm. Skills help develop new products and new ideas, which you can use to build a strong business.

If you are trying to look for ways to identify the skill that will best define your talent but are not very sure of how the internet defines it, then an excellent place to start may well be online itself. There are several platforms created to bring service providers in direct contact with buyers. These platforms are both business-to-business and freelancer-to-business platforms that can provide a great starting point to see what people are already doing online and what services could be demanded by clients. These platforms have done a very detailed job of identifying niche areas that people specialize in. Explore a few of these, and you will get a very accurate idea of how skillsets are clubbed and categorized. This initial research does not say that you must fit into any of these silos, it just gives you a starting point for your hunt of that elusive core skill around which you will create a business idea that can be offered profitably online. A few of these platforms are as follows:

- Upwork.com
- Toptal.com
- Freelancer.com
- Peopleperhour.com

I encourage you to go to these sites and look around at how they divvy up their service categories and how each service is offered on their platforms. By doing this, you can gain insight into potential business ideas as well, but we will get to that soon!

*Figure 6: Just like the foundation of a building, we need core skills to be successful.*

# Core Skills

The core skills will form the backbone of your online venture. To run a successful online venture, it needs to be supported by some critical foundation blocks: skills that are required to be successful in your venture. The supporting skills you will require are:

- Patience
- Commitment
- Humility
- Ability to research
- Being thorough
- Communication

Let me talk about each one of these and its importance in some more detail.

## Patience

Often described as the key virtue of success, this will help you tide over teething trouble and lean patches. Patience realizes there is a wait for the payoff. Waiting for something makes it more worthwhile. It will help keep things going when the times are tough and believe me; there will be times that will test you. It is critical to give yourself a timetable, to work towards achieving defined goals dedicatedly and patiently around this timetable. Patience will be the key to greater success for sure.

## Commitment

How dearly do you want to succeed? Commit to the venture wholeheartedly for a definitive chance at success. Let nothing distract you; let nothing deviate you from your goals. Nothing but a 100% commitment will be required to become a successful person. This commitment is real not only in an online venture but also for any endeavor you undertake. You do not want to be a firework entrepreneur, right?

## Humility

Humility is a virtue that helps build bridges and connections. You will need a lot of them as you go along. Be polite, keep communication channels open. Talk to various people for opportunities to learn and improve. Look for constructive feedback, both good and bad. Humility is the best way to stay connected to your market and to understand your customers. Open communication channels will also give you the much-needed help of tracking market trends and changing competition once you have an established business. Making sure that you do not talk all about yourself makes sure your clients believe that you are genuinely listening to them. Not stroking your ego and focusing others is essential to having good humility.

## Ability to Research

Learning is a journey without an end. Always try to dive deeper into your chosen field. Be on the "Know-How" bandwagon. Go above and beyond in terms of learning. Keep current on industry trends and current happenings. It is often said that a good woodcutter spends more time sharpening his ax compared to chopping wood. Believe me, and this will give lasting and impressive results over a very long time.

## Being Thorough

Customers appreciate a job well done just as much as a job done quickly. It is prudent to do a good job rather than just run after a timeline. Set realistic deadlines and then deliver exceptional work. Double-check everything. If you need to get ahold of tools that help improve quality, I recommend it. Just for example – if you want to be a writer, connect to a good dictionary and thesaurus plugin for your word processor to enhance the output you deliver. Time spent on building quality will be the most rewarding cost you can ever take up and will show as you grow at a quicker pace.

## Communication

It is essential to be a master of communication to fully show all of what you or your brand has to offer and interact appropriately with your consumer base. Every way you communicate and present yourself helps people to form an opinion on you and your brand. Wouldn't it be good to keep a positive image? Having excellent communication skills and being personable is essential to continued success.

Build a scale of 1 to 5. Try to rate yourself on the above six values on this scale. Keep investing more and more on these skills and after every time that you think tested you on any of the above. From there, you can build another rating for yourself. The higher you go on this rating scale, the better your chance of success, no matter how difficult the current situation might seem.

Here is the template I like to use:

| Skill | 1 (None) | 2 | 3 | 4 | 5 (Proficient) |
|---|---|---|---|---|---|
| Patience | | | | | |
| Commitment | | | | | |
| Humility | | | | | |
| Research Ability | | | | | |
| Being thorough | | | | | |
| Communication | | | | | |

Once you complete the chart, you can see precisely where you line up in your core skills.

If you need help improving these skills, the best way to do so is just to go out and expose yourself to experiences that put you in uncomfortable situations, like public speaking for example. To improve your presentation skills, the best way to get better is to practice over and over again. In no time, you will be a master of presenting! Likewise, with patience, call yourself out every time you start to get fidgety or distracted and take a moment to breathe and re-center yourself. The same goes for humility; call yourself out when you begin to embellish or boast. Re-center yourself and concentrate on avoiding that mistake in the future. In being thorough, it would help to develop workflows for everything you do—A list of precisely what defines a good quality output and work towards that. To improve your research ability, look up how to evaluate sources using the CRAAP test, which I will detail later in the book. As you work to develop these skills, you will not only become have a higher chance of success in any venture you undertake but also happier as well.

I know it may seem easy to read, but it is hard to bring out and practice. It will be difficult; I know that, but with persistence and focus, anything is possible.

## Skill T Chart

The things you like to do often relate to the things you do well. For example, throwing a party could show that you are a good planner or developing software shows you are a good coder. Writing letters could indicate that you are a good writer. It is easy to look and see what you are good at based on what you do best.

Invest some energy pondering what you enjoy and why—and that is your first step to where your new online career could go.

In my experiences, I have found it helpful to form a T chart, a chart or table detailing what you are good at and what you are bad at. The T Chart is the first step in finding an online venture that you would enjoy.

Below, I have included a sample T chart that you can make for your skills and talents.

| [Your Name] Skill T Chart | |
| --- | --- |
| Things I am Good At | Things I Dislike |
| • Designing Brochures<br>• Creating Websites<br>• Working with people<br>• Presenting technically | • Number Crunching<br>• Repetitive Tasks<br>• Teaching others |

On the next page, you will have room to fill out your own Skill T Chart.

| _____ Skill T Chart | |
|---|---|
| Things I am Good At | Things I Dislike |
|  |  |

# Uncovering Your Skills and Talents

After you finish the chart, pause for a minute for self-reflection and ask yourself: "What do I believe are my most prominent qualities?" Be glad—list things that you typically wouldn't say about yourself and gloat a smidgen.

One of the things that I find helps with this process is to email three individuals throughout your life whom you trust and ask them what they find most interesting about you. It can feel awkward to ask, but let them know too that you're doing some professional development and would appreciate their sentiment and criticism. I ensure you will be astounded and captivated by what you hear!

After you have finished emailing people that you trust, investigate this data you have assembled. What topics or patterns do you see? Are there any recurring themes? What have you found out about what you do well? How can you use this to help you start an online venture that you would be happy at while working?

Perhaps you have discovered that your eye for detail, insane clean work area, and the ability to dependably motivate individuals to feel great are some of the most notable qualities about yourself. Or, on the other hand, your passion for form, storytelling, and bright, comical inclination justify investigating the blogging scene?

Now I can take the T Chart a step further-- We can now connect some of those skills and talents to overarching themes. On the next page, I have attached an example modified T Chart

| [Your Name] Extended Skills Chart | |
| --- | --- |
| Things I am good at: | Applicable Industries |
| <ul><li>Designing Brochures</li><li>Creating Websites</li><li>Working with people</li><li>Presenting technically</li></ul> | <ul><li>Advertising</li><li>Marketing</li><li>Web Design</li></ul> |

Try not to feel forced to find the solution precisely right at this time—instead, enable yourself to investigate potential outcomes simply. Take a little time to determine the skills you use in your everyday life. I found myself going through this process and only really noticing that I am good at individual skills when I put attention to them. For example, I never realized how much of a motivator I was until I found myself helping my peers cheer up.

Once you have finished talking to people, noticing the skills you offer, and compiling a good list of abilities, take a deep breath! You have now furnished yourself with a guide of your strengths, skills, and talents, and you can begin genuinely considering what to do with them next.

In the next section, I am going to help you refine that list and draw conclusions from it to be able to find the online interest that can help you succeed!

# Refining your Skills List

In this section, I am going to highlight some of the ways that you can look at your skills and determine exactly how you can refine your skills into original ideas. Notice how these connect back to the core skills of any online venture!

1. Know your **niche**. Where do your skills fall? Writing? Tutoring? Video Editing? Creative? Matter of Fact? Try and draw some conclusions about what specific area you see your skills fitting into.

2. **Timing**. Time is of the essence. Do you have time to work online? When do you want to start working online? How much time a day do you want to devote to working online?

3. **Commitment**. Is it accurate to say that you are prepared to commit 100% of yourself to your new online venture? Regardless of whether you spend an hour a day or 20 hours a day working online, commitment is vital.

4. **Humility**. Be modest. Take time for yourself too! Make sure that you do not overbook yourself. Make sure you establish excellent communication with partners or clients and plan for how to do that. Open correspondence is the way to a superior working relationship.

5. **Research**. Make sure that you are up to date on market trends, the economic state, and the new happenings in your industry. A good entrepreneur is continuously reading or watching the news and staying current on their industry.

6. **Thorough**. Ensure that everything is all together and ready to go before releasing any work to a boss or client. Check twice, thrice before submitting anything. I always find myself developing a checklist before I release projects to make sure that I cover points.

Have you noticed that those qualities and questions that I am asking you to ponder relate very closely to those initial traits of successful entrepreneurs I mentioned earlier? Once again, these root qualities that are the keys to success are essential as you find the skills that you want to pursue as you start an online venture.

Once you develop a way in which you can be all of the above traits in your skills, we can move on to helping you further look into other deep level skills you have. As an aside, always keep in mind, "If you are happy with what you are doing, you will never work a single day in your life." By taking the time here to figure out what skills you have, you will not have to work a day in your life because you will enjoy what you do so much!

On the next page, you will be able to expand upon your skills chart. Feel free to use this for more brainstorming!

| _____ Extended Skill Chart | |
|---|---|
| Things I am Good At | Applicable Industries |
| | |

By following this plan, you are building a winning attitude – central to your success online and in life. Always remember to enjoy while learning. As I keep reiterating, if you are enjoying what you do, then you never have to work a day in your life. Enjoying how you spend the majority of your time will help you build a life of satisfaction and immense pleasure while also helping you build a rewarding business.

To end this journey of self-discovery and skill generation, I ask that you determine one skill that you would like to use as the foundation for creating your new online business. From your extended skills list, you can pick something that you will be able to turn into a business idea, such as 'ability to create new things,' or 'can manage many tasks at once.'

My main skill I am going to pursue:

---

In the next chapter, I will be taking this core skill a step further and helping you turn that into a power that has the potential to make you stacks of money!

# 2 IDEATING AND HONING YOUR SKILLS

The refinement – building on the core

Now that we have started talking about the skills you need, it is vital to put a structure to our efforts to build a business online. Build a timetable of things that must be done to start your business. This timeline should ideally begin 12 months in advance of your target launch date, but it can be done in as little as three weeks. Spend time building this timetable – it must cover the following:

- Discovering your core idea
- Developing your core idea
- Research time for your core idea
- Testing your business idea
- Writing your business plan and finding funding if needed
- Branding your business
- Getting the legal stuff in place – permits and licenses
- Setting up shop
- Marketing and launch of the company.

Based on this plan, we will now devote time and energy refining the skill we have chosen as our core around which the business idea and the product we will build.

The core skill that we have chosen for the extended example that we will be working with throughout this book is managing multiple things at once.

From knowing that skill, we can look at different opportunities in the current markets by taking a look at market trends, and finding what we can do to truly make a venture that will not only make you happy but work well in today's economy.

Before detailing how I came to the ideas that I created, I will first explain a little about the example we will use throughout the rest of the book and then guide you on how to develop this same idea for yourself.

The idea I chose for the rest of the book as an example is a new business will be selling 3D printed parts through an e-commerce website of its own designed for specialty custom gifts and machine parts. 3D printing is a modern and emerging technology, thus a good fit for our book.

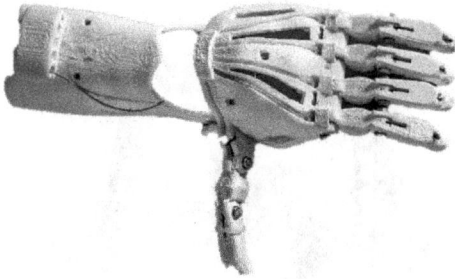

*Figure 7: An example 3D printed prosthetic*

To give a little more information on 3D printing and why it is good for us, I will discuss that briefly.

3D printing, or additive manufacturing, is the process of making a physical three-dimensional object from an electronic digital 3D model file. Through 3D printing, layers of raw material are laid down and either heated together or fused by other means to slowly build up a completed part. Each layer is a small cross-section of the part that is going to be produced. In the current scenario, 3D printing or additive manufacturing has been used in the manufacturing, medical, construction, research and development, and food industries, just to name a few. In the future, this technology will have its sociocultural impact not only on cost to produce new parts, but the ability to sustain life, reconstruct cells, and personalize everything.

*Figure 8 A 3D Printer*

The 3D Printing process is precision manufacturing that requires programmed inputs to a 3D printing machine. The business also requires understanding the needs of the clients you wish to work with, the logistics of getting the needed part moved from your production facility to the client's place of business, the financials involved, the legal permissions, and the acceptance, processing, and continued patronage of the customers. The primary sales asset will be the e-commerce website – requiring us to understand how to take credit cards online and site-building technologies. It also needs us to know how to promote our website and how we can engage better with our target audience. Since this is a relatively new and rapidly growing industry, it is ripe for entrepreneurs like us to enter!

Additionally, 3D printing has entered the world of clothing, with fashion designers experimenting with 3D-printed shoes and clothes. As an article about what 3D printing is on 3Dprinting.org adds, "In commercial production, Nike is using 3D printing to prototype and manufacture to streamline their product development process. Teachers and students have for some time been utilizing 3D printers in the classroom. 3D printing empowers understudies to emerge their ideas in a quick and interactive manner. On the off chance that you need to see 3D printing applied in the most out of control ways believable, look no farther than the aeronautic trade. From materials to idea, 3D printers are doing more and more to make planes fly and spaceships reach to the ends of the galaxy. All of this to make interstellar navigation progressively more feasible. There are quite a few designer lighting fixtures and lampshades that use 3D printing out there."

All right! Now that you know a little more about 3D printing and additive manufacturing, back to forming YOUR venture!

How do we refine the skill set we must have?
Let us start with some basics –

- Do you understand machines and computers well?
- Do you like programming?
- How good are you with business topics and management?
- How good are you with people management? Can you understand human emotion and how it affects output?

Let us build out our business idea and understand the skills required. In our concept, 3D printing allows for extreme precision part making and is thus a logical solution to machine parts that would be very hard to manufacture or are out of production.

Now the core skill you identified initially for this business was the ability to manage multiple things at one time, but the business now requires a whole lot more. While you will still be able to control various 3D printer machines, process orders, and promote the site simultaneously, there is a lot of other skills that we need to refine and develop further to ensure success. To complicate things further, the 3D printing tech space is changing rapidly, and so is the business environment. The supporting skill of "being a researcher," will come in handy for us to build this business because it will allow us to stay on top of the most prevalent market trends and economic situation.

Similarly to how I looked at all of the different facets of my example business, you should look as well with some of your potential venture ideas and think about all of the various industries, skills, and relationships you need to be successful.

I have included a form on the next few pages to be able to help you materialize some ideas, and how they interact with the industries, skills, and people you need to be successful

My Top Three Business Ideas:
- _____
- _____
- _____

Now, I invite you to look further into each idea and determine where your positions are in the respective industries.

Key Industries are the actual industries directly affected by your business idea. For example, the 3D printing company that we are using throughout the book is part of the custom gift industry, as well as the manufacturing industry. While this idea seems as though it could be scaled up very quickly to a multimillion-dollar company, we will first start with smaller custom orders and slowly grow, but I digress. I am getting ahead of myself here! I will go into much more detail on this tactic later on in the book as we further flesh out this idea.

One of the topics that I want to touch on here briefly is the meaning of a niche. A niche is a particular segment of an industry. It is a small, very specialized part of a bigger market, such as people who are interested in model railroading or people who are interested in fitness. In these niches, people are generally more inclined to buy custom products for their specific wants and needs. If you choose a niche to pursue, it would be essential to get to know their needs correctly and develop a product or service that fully satisfies their needs.

The Key People are the people that are directly affected by your business. These people could be your customers, competitors, suppliers, distributors, shipping companies, or any other person that you will need to interact with to be able to make your business successful. In the case of our idea, we will need to interact with the customer, engineers, and makers to be able to custom design the devices that we would produce. Additionally, we would need to communicate at some point with a material supplier, and a 3D printer salesman or advisor that would be able to help you choose the right machine.

The Key Skills in the business are what are essential, especially at this step. This step will tell you whether your skills genuinely correspond with the idea you came up with. You will want to spend a considerable amount of time thinking of every skill that you would need to be able to be proficient at to run the business successfully. In our case, there are many skills that we would need such as the ability to program and operate a 3D printer, model devices in computer-aided design software, ship and pack orders, manage finances, create workflows to ensure quality, present and sell to clients, and develop a website to sell the parts. As you can see, there are many more skills here than directly apparent, so it is essential to think and understand the idea in all regards.

On the next page, I invite you to write out what I was detailing for all of the ideas you are considering. By doing this, you will be able to find the ideas that come naturally to you and what you would typically be better at.

Business Idea:

_____

Key **Industries** and how they help us:

- _____
- _____
- _____
- _____
- _____

Key **People** and how they help us:

- _____
- _____
- _____
- _____
- _____

Key **Skills** we need to interact with key people and industries:

- _____
  - o   How it helps our key people or industries:

_____

- _____
  - o   How it helps our key people or industries:

_____

- _____
  - o   How it helps our key people or industries:

_____

- _____
  - o   How it helps our key people or industries:

Business Idea:

_____

Key **Industries** and how they help us:

- _____
- _____
- _____
- _____
- _____

Key **People** and how they help us:

- _____
- _____
- _____
- _____
- _____

Key **Skills** we need to interact with key people and industries:

- _____
  - How it helps our key people or industries:

_____

- _____
  - How it helps our key people or industries:

_____

- _____
  - How it helps our key people or industries:

_____

- _____
  - How it helps our key people or industries:

Business Idea:

Key **Industries** and how they help us:

- _____
- _____
- _____
- _____
- _____

Key **People** and how they help us:

- _____
- _____
- _____
- _____
- _____

Key **Skills** we need to interact with key people and industries:

- _____
  - How it helps our key people or industries:

_____

- _____
  - How it helps our key people or industries:

_____

- _____
  - How it helps our key people or industries:

_____

- _____
  - How it helps our key people or industries:

## Learning New Skills

Nobody is perfect. Nobody knows everything. Through the self-discovery in chapter one and the business idea analysis presented here in chapter two, hopefully, you were able to find some skills that need a little bit of work. As for the Core Success skills I mentioned in chapter one, just experience them! For other skills that are more technical and cannot be learned directly by experience or self-reflection, you will need to be able to learn in the more traditional sense.

To learn a new skill or to upgrade your existing skills. Nothing matches up to going back to college or the training center that specializes in that field. Join a business class that gives a jump start in managing a business, or take a coding class to learn how to program that next great app. This said, I must emphasize that a formal course is not the only way of learning the skill you need. There are a host of other options available that help skill upgrades at a pace that you are comfortable with as well as a cost you are comfortable with.

Join online forums, become a member of a learning site, or even talk to someone in the field and see if they would let you be their apprentice!

If you want to take the more traditional skill-building process, I will list a few ways that have worked well in the past to learn new skills:

*Figure 9: There are many places to learn... Including the traditional classroom!*

# Places to Learn

There are many places where you can learn new skills and refine the skills you already have. In the digital world, there are not only a lot of in-person opportunities but also online options that allow you to be able to work at your own pace and difficulty. Depending on your schedule and time commitment, many options are available for you to learn.

## In-Person Learning

By far, this is the best way to learn something. You will be able to learn directly from people who are experts in the field and be able to ask questions directly and get instant detailed feedback from your professor or instructor. Some of the drawbacks of this type of instruction are that there is generally a set schedule, a time commitment on a daily basis, and structured exams and reinforcement for the class. Of the types of learning I will detail, this type of education will allow you to truly become a master of the skill you want to learn.

## Online Learning

A new way of learning that has increased incredibly recently is learning new skills online. Some platforms allow experts in the field to be able to create their own online 'courses' focused around a central skill like web development or data analytics. There are many platforms on the internet like Udemy that allow you to pay only a few dollars to gain access to a plethora of content and ways to learn. In this type of learning, you can set up your own schedule and have more of a laid-back style of presentation. It is not as high stress as in-person learning, because you do not get graded on any assignment and do not necessarily have access to the instructor to learn from directly. Additionally, many people mention that it is very easy to get distracted when learning online due to our computers being the place where we also take care of business and have fun as well.

## Alternative Learning Ways

In a lot of different niches, there are specific learning websites or communities that allow you to learn directly from experts in the field. Look up some of the communities around the niche or industry that you have chosen to pursue. Many communities have a list of links that link to great informational websites that can teach you a lot about your skills.

Forums also exist for almost every different industry where people can gather online and talk about industry trends or share tutorials they have made. Forums are also a great place to get help for any hard to solve issues that you have been having. Through this way, you can reach out directly to people who know what they are doing and have plenty of experience in your industry.

Additionally, a popular video streaming service that almost everyone uses is YouTube. If you have a particular question, chances are someone has made a video answering it or a tutorial on how to do something. Video tutorials are beneficial to someone, especially as you run into issues developing a product, or creating a program. Some YouTube tutorials will be able to show you precisely what you are trying to learn or fix.

One example that I have of this phenomenon was when my grandfather, who was a tradesman and mechanic, did not know how to properly disassemble the supercharger of his car to replace a part internal to the unit. Through the power of YouTube, he was able to find the exact model supercharger's disassembly video and reverse engineered what was wrong with the unit from the video. That goes to show the sheer amount of content and possibilities to improve your skills that there is on this free open market to learn.

## Open Courses

Another cross between college learning and online learning is an exciting initiative by the Massachusetts Institute of Technology called OpenCourseWare. OpenCourseWare is a great program that I highly recommend that makes the lecture of popular MIT courses open to anyone to view. Although it does not allow you to contact the professor or get feedback, it is an excellent middle-ground to online learning and in-person learning. Since you can take your time learning skills and still have access to some of the worksheets and reinforcement exercises that allow you to learn the material well.

Additionally, there are some perks for the older generation among us. Many community colleges allow you to audit classes free of charge if you are above a certain age. Auditing a class will enable you to go to class and learn the material but not get a grade for the course. While this does not formally validate your knowledge, it is undoubtedly a great way to learn free of charge!

## Apprenticeships

One of the last ways I wanted to touch on is an apprenticeship. If you are dead set on doing something incredibly specific and targeted, there is no better way to learn than from learning directly from a master in the field and be able to determine exactly what you learn from them. If you know a master in the industry you wish to pursue or in the skill that you want to improve, I would not hesitate to write them an email asking them if they would be willing to teach an apprentice or even sit down for a coffee and talk for an hour. Time with a master in the craft is incredibly beneficial if you want to be able to learn some industry best practices.

## Getting a Mentor

I have had some challenging learning experiences in my search for the right business mentors. By the word "mentor," I mean anyone you choose to learn from: teachers, coaches, business team leaders, authors, experts, or colleagues.

Before you go out there seeking the advice of others, take some time to get to know what you desire in not only your business venture but your mentor as well. What is most important to you in your business success?

What is most important to me in my business success?

_____

Next, create a list of the most important qualities and areas of expertise that you want your mentors to have. Be clear about you want, and then it will be much easier to find it!

Qualities I want in a mentor:

- _____
- _____

- _____
- _____
- _____

I have discovered over time that I need business mentors who have exceptional integrity, who empower and inspire me, who facilitate the deepening of my connection with my sense of truth,  people who are not afraid to be direct and truthful. I learned all this mostly by not finding it in previous mentors! I was being disappointed over and over again until I learned to be more transparent in knowing what I needed and going after it.

Before you reach out to someone, first take some time to learn about the person you want to learn from. Learn about their background, credentials, and experience. For example, if you are going to learn about how to set up a successful soap-making business, you will want to find someone who has made soap before and knows the tips and tricks of the trade. They would be most suited to teach you about the small details that come from experience.

What do I want to learn from my mentor?

- _____
- _____
- _____

The more closely you intend to work with someone, the more carefully you will want to check out that person to make sure there is a good fit. If you're going to be in a long-term coaching relationship, it is essential that you communicate with your potential business mentor to ensure that you work well together.

Also, I encourage you to think about the following questions:

- Do you feel inspired, empowered, and uplifted from your prospective mentor's teachings?
- Do you feel more connected with your own inner sense of truth from their teachings?
- Does your prospective business mentor walk their talk? Do they practice what they preach? Do they follow their own advice, use the products they sell, and embody and express the principles they are talking about?
- Does their "energy" match their words? For example, if a coach is speaking about the importance of holding a positive attitude towards others, do you experience this positive attitude actually coming from them? Or do their words say one thing, but their energy conveys something else?

Before taking the advice of anyone, always ask your intuition and your inner sense of truth. Use discernment to navigate through the sea of information on the internet, to find business mentors of integrity and wisdom that can empower you to success. Trust your instincts, avoid hype, and set your intention to create business success!

From there, I hope you have developed a few people you have considered to mentor you. I encourage you to write them below.

Name: _____

Email: _____

Name: _____

Email: _____

Name: _____

Email: _____

## Crafting an Introduction Email

Many people may be wondering, why craft an introduction email for this? I am just asking for their help. I have calculated this section very carefully. Think about it. If someone is not able to respond to an introduction email, how useful would they be working to mentor us in a *technologically* facing company? I ultimately see the value in phone calls and face to face communication, but this simple task will help screen people to be a coach in ways that work wonders. Below, I have a simple outline for an email that I have used in the past to get connected with someone in the industry to form a mentor-apprentice relationship.

1. Greet the person you are writing
    a. Make sure to be formal in this, and make sure that your email doesn't appear spammy.
2. Introduce yourself
    a. Make sure you mention:
        i. Where you are from
        ii. Your interests
        iii. What you are hoping to do (Build a business, right!?)
3. Compliment the person you are writing
    a. Mention some work of theirs that connected with you or your career goals
    b. Mention an accomplishment of theirs and say how it is something you hope to accomplish one day
4. Explain what you want from them.
    a. Do you want to get coffee with them?
    b. Do you want to video chat with them?
    c. Do you want to form a business relationship?
    d. What do you want to learn?
5. Call them to action
    a. Ask them to call you or email you to follow up
    b. Let them know your availability

    c.   Please mention that you can work around their schedule to find a time that works for both of you

6.   Thank them for their time
    a.   Make sure to be kind—they are doing a favor to you!

7.   Sign the email without any company signatures.
    a.   By making sure you don't use a prebuilt email signature, the message seems more genuine to the recipient.

If you do not hear back from the person you emailed, make sure to follow up after a week. If it is someone who would be available for a phone call, at this point, I would then call them. When you do hear back, try to firm up plans to get coffee or chat online to start and see where it goes from there.

## Questions to Ask Your Mentor

When you get around to speaking to your mentor in person or online, make sure to ask them insightful questions that you can learn a lot from.

- What is it like in our industry?
- How have you been able to grow within the industry?
- Are there any professional certifications that are essential to our industry?
- What are some little-known tips and tricks on our field?
- Also, be sure to ask industry-specific questions and things you want to know as well. Be sure you pick their brain for all knowledge on how to succeed in the industry when you sit down with them.

One thing that always works for me is having a predetermined list of questions that I can go into a meeting with jotted down in a beautiful folio or notebook, spaced enough to where I can add their response under the prompt.

Furthermore, I always leave a section in my notebook for simple, one-liner words of wisdom that I have learned from them that I can reference easily.

This section, by no measure, is an exhaustive one. Research the web, and you will find many resources that can help you gain the knowledge you need for your new venture. The only rule we advise is to approach a credible learning source for getting the best and the very latest of what you require. Web Research is especially essential with any form of programming, to make sure you are getting non-obsolete or end of life information.

To find useful articles in the programming sphere, I always make sure to look up the most recent of whatever package I work with, say Python or PHP, and this way I can include that software version on my searches to make sure that I am getting only the most recent information.

For a budding computer modeler that will be working with CAD software, the learning can be a daunting task. When you are ready to start, there are just hundreds of resources through video tutorials, software demonstrations, and manufacturer documentation to be able to get you started quickly learning the ropes. With our business in creating prosthetic parts, we will need to learn CAD software as well as how to properly operate the machines we will one day own.

In order to be successful in this field, we are going to want to connect with the maker community, even potential prosthetic doctors or surgeons that are able to provide insight into the industry and where to start. From there, we can find out the needs of our industry and which skills we need to improve in order to be successful. By doing this research now, we will be able to take a risk more accurately and calculatedly by opening our online business.

Skills I want to improve:

- _____
- _____
- _____
- _____
- _____
- _____
- _____
- _____
- _____
- _____

# Building a Business Launch Plan

This entire skills upgrade process must be helping us form our business launch plan. Let me delve a little into the process of creating the launch plan. Two essential components of building this plan come from the ability to research and the skill of humility, as we discussed as two of the core skills for any successful entrepreneur in chapter one. By research, you will be able to understand the latest trends that have a direct impact on your business idea or are likely to impact your business later. The other important point is to identify roadblocks and then plan ways to overcome them. Overcoming roadblocks is achieved through proper brainstorming.

Building a business launch timeline can be done with support from online resources. Creating your launch plan is a detailed activity; spend a lot of quality time learning how to do this and then doing it in elaborate detail for your business. Time spent here will save you much trouble later, making this a critical activity for the business going forward. It is vital to make sure that you at least have this document created to complete the rest of the book successfully. Everything does not need to be filled out at this point, only the first checkbox, which we completed in Chapter One by evaluating the strengths and weaknesses we face. On the next page, I will detail the checklist, and I encourage you to copy this document into a binder for you to have at your disposal.

I have not included due dates on these items. Instead, I have just laid them out for you because it seems everyone would like to take a different timeline to launch their venture.

## INITIAL STEPS:
- ☐ Assess your strengths and weaknesses.
- ☐ Determine how you could improve your strengths and downplay your weaknesses
- ☐ Determine the best way to commercialize the skills you identified.

## FEASIBILITY ANALYSIS
- ☐ Determine the startup costs of your business
- ☐ Talk to customers directly to validate your need
- ☐ Determine if you have the financials available to take on this new venture.
  - o Talk to a lender or family and friends (If Needed)

## RESEARCH
- ☐ Determine company legal entity type
- ☐ Determine company hierarchy
- ☐ Research Insurance needs
- ☐ Market Research
  - o Identify and research your ideal customer
  - o Identify competitors
  - o Identify competitor strengths and weaknesses
  - o Look at Industry trends

**PLAN**

- ☐ Create your business plan
- ☐ Create a marketing plan
- ☐ Prepare legal paperwork
- ☐ Obtain all permits needed
- ☐ Make sure all proper licensing is taken care of
- ☐ Open a business bank account
- ☐ Find a Lawyer
- ☐ Find an Insurance Agent
- ☐ Find an accountant

BUILD

- ☐ Set up your recordkeeping software
- ☐ Familiarize yourself with the tax structure of your chosen entity type
- ☐ Obtain a lease (If Needed)
- ☐ Find Suppliers
- ☐ Buy All necessary equipment
- ☐ Build your product or service and all associated management tools
- ☐ Review all documents with your attorney before you sign them.

**NETWORK**

- ☐ Get Business Cards
- ☐ Join groups of likeminded individuals
- ☐ Create or update your LinkedIn account or personal website.
- ☐ Set a start date

**FINISH**

- ☐ Sign all legal documents
- ☐ Make sure products are ready

- ☐ Launch marketing campaign
- ☐ Determine tasks that need to be completed every day, week, month, and year.
- ☐ Perform a soft launch

## LAUNCH

- ☐ Tell everyone you know what you are doing!
- ☐ Launch part 2 of your social media plan
- ☐ Start doing your daily operations and usual

## MANAGE

- ☐ Do the tasks you outlined
- ☐ Stay up to date on market trends
- ☐ Stay competitive

To resolve various issues you will encounter right from the time you start making the plan will require much brainstorming. Whether you plan to build a business on your own or have a team, a business will need problem-solving at every stage, and you will have to accept humility and ask people that you trust for their point of view. Just for an example – for the 3D printing business, the question you need an answer to may be as simple as how to get rid of this finicky error on your printer. Luckily, you can use an online forum to get ideas, but again this will require working with other people and brainstorming. Thus, it pays to study the technique of brainstorming right at the start and use it effectively as a problem-solving tool throughout your business and life's journey.

# Brainstorming

Creativity or inventiveness is a virtue that we as a whole have hidden within us. It includes the yearn to discover or innovate of something new or the re-development of something previously existing to make it valuable or interesting.

Some people seem to have surface-level creativity, while other Individuals state that their inventiveness or creativity is intrinsic. For other people, communicating inventiveness takes additional time and development. One essential point to understand is that all of us are able to be inventive. Finding it inside of you is easier than you think. In order to unlock the inventiveness inside of you, I recommend you attempt the following:

# 1. Change your viewpoint.

You may have heard the expression "Think fresh". You should have a go at taking a gander at the circumstances from an alternate perspective.

Change your point of view. Consider all factors that are influenced by your concern or your anxiety. Attempt to breakdown the issue into a few components at that point mix them. Have you ever contemplated on the consequences if a component or part is substituted? However, this area is essential in working on your inventiveness since it encourages you get rid of potential obsessions that may frustrate innovativeness.

## 2. Intellectually change your present location.

Envision how someone else would respond if they were faced within a similar circumstance. Imagine how different conditions would work when managing a similar issue. Application in various settings can be additionally done, and afterward from that point, adjust the answer for the current environment.

## 3. Think outside the box.

Exercise and Engage your creative mind. Adjustment can trigger inventiveness since you see things from an alternate or different perspective. Nevertheless, attempt to overstate or think about your ideas in a different way to force your mind to think within different boundaries, be it amplification or minimization of any one part of an idea. contemplating about the potential contrasts between these two circumstances could create thoughts. Try different solutions to exercise your brain!

## 4. Get Comfy.

When brainstorming, you need a good, conducive, and enabling environment. It would be best if you had some place you can be without being superfluously upset so you can give an issue your complete consideration and attention. Your environment ought to stretch out to the individuals you are around. You will in general improve at something when you are with similarly invested individuals. To lay it out plainly, spend time with innovative individuals to help improve your inventive capacities.

More often, individuals will in general be progressively imaginative when they are with individuals who are doing likewise. Research has also shown that on the off chance that you wish to be increasingly imaginative, you try and be around people with the same goals in mind.

## 5. Time, time, time.

Creativity need not be rushed. Therefore, the idea of coming up with a fast solution or generally being fast does not help in the flow of thoughts. Your psyche will in general go into a condition of slight confusion when you are attempting to force or drive things in. Studies indicate that ideas created in this state are commonly low quality or unused. In the event that you don't have a lot of time, keep a reference list of some ideas you had to reference later. Go through all the different permutations, orientations, positions, arrangements, and organizations of the ideas in your mind and ensure that you try all of them and allocate time to it, and give each one a shot.

## 6. Get help from others and see what they think

Having someone else look at this problem from a different perspective can help immensely. Allow for many different perspectives! Never hesitate to ask the question "why?". In school, I was always taught to use the 'five why's' to determine the root pain point or problem in order to fix the source of the issue. This is simply asking why something the way it is five times back. Furthermore, having diversity in coming up with solutions is beneficial for creativity. Get a time together to generate new ideas. Bouncing ideas off of other people allow you to get on the same metaphorical path and can allow even more accessory ideas to arise. The unconstrained nature of these new thoughts helps in detailing of more thoughts that could potentially lead you to a final solution. The results of this brainstorming session can be the crude material in the development of your full-fledged idea!

Recall that in conceptualizing, four methods are to be adhered to for it to be said to a success: It should be devoid of criticisms.

- Criticism blocks the endless flow of inspirational thoughts and ideas.
- Criticism can be delayed or put on hold until this session is over.
- Combining ideas and modifying thoughts are also welcomed. In brainstorming, quantity is favored over quality
- Abnormal or unusual thoughts are encouraged.

These are only a few steps you need to take to get your inventive energies moving. They can be adjusted to suit every person.

A lot of it is down to you. How innovative would you be able to be? How open right?

Expel the limits from your brain and you will discover your innovativeness will increase.

## Additional Information

Many online resources are available for this as well; a few we found interesting are as follows:

- https://coschedule.com/blog/brainstorming-techniques/ https://www.wrike.com/blog/techniques-effective-brainstorming/
- https://www.mindtools.com/brainstm.html

Once you have refined your skills and built a business launch plan, you will gain much confidence in how things will happen. You will also have a lot more control over this process to ensure that they move forward at a pace you have set for yourself. This plan will also be a reality check – it will keep you focused and goal-driven, ensuring that you face little or no distraction.

I continue to emphasize the importance of skill development and the supporting skills when venturing out on your own. Working with people, as well as regulatory compliance, is as important as being able to work with technology. Thus, building on each skill is critical and must not be sidelined.

## Good Launch Plan Criteria

The Launch Plan gets you ready for forming not only your professional development but will also be used later in the book to help you launch your business.

Is the Launch Plan:

*Complete?* Does it list all the action steps or changes to be looked for in every single significant piece of the group (e.g., schools, business, government, confidence group)?

*Clear?* Is it obvious who will do what by when?

*Current?* Does the activity design mirror the present work? Does it envision recently rising openings and obstructions?

Be specific and realistic in your planning.

Having a particular objective is only the starting point: you should be specific and reasonable in each part of your undertaking — for instance, by expressing distinct and achievable calendars, goals, and ultimate results.

Planning for hiccups is also helpful. What is Plan B? C? D? Just making sure that there is something in place to help you recover from a disappointment may be the difference between completing the next goal on time or being behind on your plan.

Example: To get the 3D printer set up for our business, we first need to have a table to put it on. Before we can get a table to put it on, we need to make sure that there is an area near an outlet that we can use to make sure that the printer will get power. In short, we need to be sure that we take every individual step in the process into account.

What I am trying to explain here is to make sure that you are laying out all of the prerequisites that you need to accomplish before you can get the business launched—That is the entire purpose of the launch plan. Setting goals to keep you focused and started is essential to this process.

## Keep a Record of Everything

As you work through your ideation process, keep notes of everything. I like to call this my Journal. You may think that it's pointless to have a notebook with various tabs in it to segment off multiple parts of your action plan, but I assure you it will not only give your life a better direction, but it will help as you work to start your eVenture and will aid you immensely when you start filing for patent protection, trademarks, and other forms of intellectual property protection.

Tabbed sections I have in my action plan binder are:
- Ideas/Miscellaneous notes
- Daily Schedules
- Monthly Schedules
- Milestones
- Research
- Contacts

Another essential part of this process is making sure that everything is dated and trackable. There are some software packages out there that will allow you to keep track of all of your notes in virtual 'binders,' but I highly recommend using pencil and paper for this initial step, so that you can get the satisfaction of crossing items off of the list and your data is not accessible by others except yourself. I am sure this is a tad of me being paranoid about data security, but making sure that you are the only one accessing your critical business information is essential in this day and age. One drawback of having all of this on pencil and paper is that there is no cloud backup if anything goes awry, but you will have to weigh the options and see what is right for you.

## Forming Your Business Idea

In developing the ideas for your business, staying up with the latest with industry news and patterns will enable you to pick up involvement, recognize open doors for development, and give you a focused edge.

Remaining on top of changes and practices in your industry should not be troublesome. However – just perused our tips underneath and figured out how you can get your next million-dollar business idea!

To help us form great business ideas, you can take these steps:

## 1. Talk to a mentor or industry advisor

As I have mentioned in this chapter, having coffee with a mentor or companion who has involvement in your industry will enable you to learn new data in a social setting. It is invaluable to be able to get real industrial feedback and help you formulate a business idea. Having the capacity to make inquiries without judgment is the way to building your insight on your industry and seeing things from another viewpoint.

I will talk to: _____

## 2. Distinguish your Company Vision.

Using the skills you have mapped out in the last chapter, think about some cool things that you can do and what your advisor has mentioned to you and formulate a company vision plan. A company vision is a statement that describes the short- or long-term goals of a company.

My Company Vision:

_____

_____

_____

_____

_____

## 3. Remain hungry for learning.

Your current thoughts are never enough, and you are never done learning. I find myself learning something new every day and becoming more and more knowledgeable in a variety of different areas.

In this way, we remain up and coming on what is happening in your industry and utilize those bits of knowledge to form a good business idea. Adhere profoundly to the vision or mission for your business, yet, keep an open mind to other occurrences in your industry as well. Else, you hazard being deserted and passing up an excellent opportunity for the open doors delighted in by your opposition.

## 4. Think about where you stand

Look back on your skills. Take a look at where all of your skills line up and how can you improve. If you need to learn new skills, check out earlier in Chapter two for ways you can learn new skills on a budget. With courses now being offered on the web and at a low cost, you can keep on working while at the same time expanding your knowledge base or take a business or IT course that could be pertinent to a wide variety of online ventures.

## 5. Stay Informed

A free and straightforward approach to remain on top of your industry is to sign up for online blogs, news platforms, and industry reviews conveyed straight to your inbox. Every industry has a general forum for people to discuss news, topics, and share their recent accomplishments. I would highly recommend creating an account and checking out some of the topics. An excellent way to find this is by searching Google for '[Industry Name] forum,' and you are bound to find one. If there is not one, it may be a good idea to start one! If you discover an absence of time and a jumbled inbox is preventing you from perusing your news, take a stab at printing them out or utilizing a reader application to be able to see the most recent news on your mobile device. Get into the routine of reading them in the morning during breakfast every day, and you will slowly become more literate on the trends and change factors in your industry.

## 6. Learn from others in the industry

See how people in the industry are interacting with each other. See what the client's dissatisfactions with current products on the market are. Try and work to make something better than that. That is a lot to think about, but at this point, that is all we have to do; get the gears in your mind turning and thinking of new ways to

## 7. Network

Get yourself out of the workplace to go to meetings, industry occasions, and instructional courses. Contact providers, clients, and experts who work in related fields to get a more extensive comprehension of your industry. Networking with new individuals may likewise stay up with the latest with your rivals' reasoning, which can be used to help your own business and, ultimately, your bottom line.

My Business Idea

_____

_____

_____

_____

# 3 RESEARCHING YOUR MARKET

Doing your homework – when the rubber hits the road

It is essential to gather as much information about your market as you can before you start your business. The research should help you figure out if there is a demand for your product or service. A detailed competitive analysis can help in refining margins and pricing your product or service. It should help you set up your business at the right location and also in creating a plan to differentiate your offering.

Doing your due diligence while researching your market can mean the difference between a successful business and a loss of money and time. The best part about all of this is that doing excellent market research does not need to cost a ton. Doing simple things like researching online, creating focus groups, networking, and surveys can help you study your market.

To highlight what proper market research can do, we have this example of a company that offers pet accessories online. The company started selling accessories such as collars, leashes, and pet food bowls through an online site. They were doing well, but customers would only order from them once and would not order again. The owner of the company wanted to learn why. This is where the research comes to the rescue. The owner of the company sent out a survey to all of his customers. It asked a plethora of questions about their service offerings, products, and customer service. From the survey, he learned that people wanted customized products, bowls, collars, and leashes with their pet's name on it. Today, they have seen significant growth in their business because of this research.

We have already covered what comes before the research – a strong business idea. Once the basic idea is in place, we do a complete activity to validate it and to understand that it is viable. To figure out if you should go ahead with your business idea, you need to ask questions like these (Feel free to write in the margins!):

- Is there a lot of compeition?

  _____

- How much money is spent in your industry each year in your area?

  _____

- Is there room in the market for one more business?

  _____

- Does the market want what you are offering?

  _____

To highlight a few points - Or if you are developing a new online service for day traders, is it something they cannot live without? Will anyone care?

What is the competition doing?

_____
_____
_____
_____
_____
_____

What do they do well?

_____
_____
_____
_____
_____

What do they do poorly?

_____
_____
_____
_____
_____

What is unique about them?

_____
_____
_____
_____
_____

- Can you offer something different that will encourage customers to come to you instead of more established businesses?

_____

_____

_____

_____

_____

_____

- How can you reach your target audience?

_____

_____

_____

_____

_____

- Are you specializing in an area with a population of the right age and disposable income?

_____

_____

_____

_____

_____

_____

Once you have validated the business idea, it is time to get into the details. Go much deeper into how you will create a business and what will be your competitive advantage. Your competitive advantage is essential to making sure that you are different from every other company in your field. You need information that will help you develop a unique business proposition that will give you a significant competitive advantage.

*Figure 10: Doing adequate research now can save you a headache later!*

# Your Target Market

Knowing for whom your product is designed for is called knowing your target market. Your target market is the pinpointed group for whom you are building this product. It is essential to find out whom you want to sell to and nail this group down early in the process to avoid wasted time and effort. By doing this now, you can gain a better understanding of the market and design to that.

# Knowing your Customer

Knowing your customers is essential to ensure the success of a business. You need it to be able to survive. Knowing your customers is different from knowing what they buy. Understanding how they feel, what they need, what they want, and what they desire can prove to be helpful when developing a product that exactly satisfies their needs.

By knowing your customer, this will naturally guide us into validating the idea and developing a user-centered product or service.

Make sure you develop your target market thoroughly by asking the following questions:

## Who makes the market of a product?

Determining who makes the product corresponds back to the core of the business: whom we are designing our product for? Our target market is the answer.

What age are they?

_____

What gender are they?

_____

Where do they live?

_____

How much do they make?

_____

Are there any other unique qualifiers for your target audience?

_____

## What do people buy?

Now that we know who our clients are, we need to examine how they buy. We should understand what they need to survive and why they buy.

What does your target audience buy?

Daily?

● _____

- _____
- _____
- _____
- _____

Monthly?

- _____
- _____
- _____
- _____
- _____

Yearly?

- _____
- _____
- _____
- _____
- _____

Once?

- _____
- _____
- _____
- _____
- _____

## Why do people buy?

Now that we understand what they need, we must examine why they need it.

What motivates our target audience?

_____
_____
_____
_____

How do they control their impulse buying?

_____

_____

_____

_____

What qualities of a product are most important to them?

_____

_____

_____

_____

How do they choose which product is better?

_____

_____

_____

_____

## Who is influential in the buying decision?

Now that we understand why they buy, we need to know who influences the buying decision. In some cases, it may only be the one single person that makes a decision. In many business to business products, more than one person is making the final decision.

Who influences the decision-maker?

_____

_____

_____

What is their role?

_____

What are their motivations?

How do they communicate with the decision-maker?

What stake do they have in the final decision?

## Who makes the buying decision?

Understanding who actually purchases the product can tell you a lot about what methods are the best way to reach your target audience. Make sure to ponder the following questions:

Who purchases the product?

What is their title?

What is their primary motivator for making this purchase?

What would make your product more desirable to them?

How can I reach their interests?

_____

_____

_____

What forms of technology do they use?

_____

_____

_____

_____

## When do people buy?

After we find who makes this decision, we need to see when that decision to buy is made. By understanding when the decision is made, we can tailor our advertising for a particular time of the year.

Is there a time of year this product is bought?

_____

How often does a target user purchase your product?

_____

Are there any events that trigger the purchase?

_____

Is the purchase triggered by someone else?

_____

## Where do people buy?

Now that we know when people buy, we need to understand where people buy the product. Understanding where people buy the product will let us know how we can effectively distribute our product to take advantage of the sources our target market utilizes the most.

Where is the product sold?

_____

How is it delivered?

What is the process of selling look like?

_____

_____

_____

_____

How customized is the process of getting the product?

_____

_____

_____

_____

How much support needs to be provided?

_____

Is there any way we can distribute our product differently, but effectively?

_____

_____

_____

_____

_____

Marketing research relies on other sciences as well, such as psychology or sociology. Being able to develop the products consumers need, and then market them following the consumers' behavior lay the basis for competitive advantages and shape the strategic decisions a business must make.

## Who uses the product?

Who is the primary user of the product?

_____

Is it the same as the selling target market?

_____

What are their concerns?

_____

_____

_____

_____

What do they expect out of your product?

_____

_____

_____

_____

How can you satisfy those expectations when you are designing your product?

_____

_____

_____

_____

_____

# Developing a proto persona

A proto persona is an example ideal customer. Your proto persona is the embodification of your target market. This persona is a metaphorical fake person who would be interested in the product. In the User Experience industry, this is a significant step in creating a user-centered design, but I feel this can be interpreted to businesses in general.

| Information: | Behavior: |
|---|---|
| Name: | Buying Habits: |
| Age: | Goals: |
| Skills: | |
| Technological Affinity: | |
| **Pain Points:** | **Solutions to their problems:** |
| | |

# Interpreting the Results

From this initial target market research, you may be wondering how you can take this information and make it into a real product.

I encourage you to think about how you can apply this information to your business idea. How do you use the information herein your concept? Since there is so much information here and at this point, every business idea should be unique, but I will leave it up to you and your critical thinking skills to adequately interpret and find the use in your target market information.

# Standard Information to Research

Information that you need will often depend on the type of business you are planning to get into and the circumstances of the case, but options include the following:

## Trade Information

Trade information is best obtained by reading publications of the trade association like its website, or its magazine and white papers or research papers. You can also spend time visiting trade shows and exhibitions and talk to many people already in this line of business.

Trade Journals in my Industry:

- _____
- _____
- _____

## Demographic and Economic Data

Try the U.S. Census Bureau's Website, State Census information, or most recent Economic Census to find demographic data like age range, income, or number of businesses by type in a geographic area

One piece of information that is helpful to know is that your local library generally has a ton of resources available to you on researching your local area. Another source of information could be your local chamber of commerce and can guide you on the road for more information you could need it.

Target Market Details:

- Age Range: _____
- Average Income: _____
- Disposable Income? _____
- Total Sales in Niche? _____

## Local Business Groups

Your local chamber of commerce may be able to help you find more information on your local area. Also, try government-sponsored Small Business Development Centers. These centers assist entrepreneurs and small-business owners with starting and growing their businesses. Local governments what you to succeed—it helps their local economy and secures their job!

Business Groups in my Target Market:

- _____
- _____
- _____
- _____
- _____

## Local Universities

Sometimes professors at business schools are interested in having their students do a market feasibility study for course credit as part of business course curriculum. Contacting a local university is an excellent option if you are tight on cash. These students have access to thousands of dollars in market research and industry analysis and will give you a very solid product.

Local Universities:

- _____
- _____
- _____
- _____
- _____

## Local Competitors

If you are starting a business focused in a localized area, shop the competition and check their websites. Determine what they are doing and how you can be different. In another sense, find a similar business in a similar city and ask to talk to the owner. Also, look for related businesses for sale and contact the brokers for information like why they are selling and the financials of the business. You may even be interested in buying that business yourself.

Local Competitors:

- _____
- _____
- _____
- _____
- _____

## National Competitors

Do an online search of large businesses in your industry and evaluate what they offer to help fine-tune your idea. Every sector has some form of a national syndicate that is dominating the market.

National Competitors:

- _____
- _____
- _____
- _____
- _____
- _____
- _____
- _____
- _____
- _____

## Potential Customers

Making sure that you talk to potential customers is essential to making sure you hit the nail on the head when researching your market. Talk with friends of friends--but not your friends or family, since they may not tell you the truth—and any old customers or existing customers, if you're already in business, can offer you a proper perspective as well. Testing with unknown people is the acid test to see if your plan is ready for prime time or needs tweaking.

All your efforts spent on research will pay you rich dividends, either by helping you validate your business plan, sending you back to the drawing board, or convincing you to shelve it altogether. Do not worry if you seem to have all the information needed to tell you this is a bad idea; it is much better to find that now rather than later! If that happens, I encourage you to restart the process again around another top business idea.

*Figure 11: You do not need to 'roll the dice' to see if a source is valid with this test!*

# CRAAP Test

The CRAAP Test is a way of determining the legitimacy of a source you are using in your research. Many people may be wondering why I would cover this, but it is essential to talk about this during the research process. In the digital world, there is plenty of great information, but due to the ease of being able to publish on the internet, there is misinformation as well, especially in breaking news stories. The CRAAP test provides a list of questions for you to ask yourself when you evaluate the legitimacy of a source. California State University in Chico has a great handout on this. I have modified this guide slightly and included it below.

## Currency

The timeliness of the information.

- When was the information published or posted?
- Has the information been revised or updated?
- Does your topic require current information, or will older sources work as well?
- Are the links functional? Relevance: The importance of the information for your needs.

## Relevance

The importance of the information for your needs

- Does the information relate to your topic or answer your question?
- Who is the intended audience?
- Is the information at an appropriate level (i.e., not too elementary or advanced for your needs)?
- Have you looked at a variety of sources before determining this is one you will use?
- Would you be comfortable citing this source in your research paper?

## Authority

The Source of the Information

- Who is the author/publisher/source/sponsor?
- What are the author's credentials or organizational affiliations?
- Is the author qualified to write on the topic?

- Is there contact information, such as a publisher or email address?
- Does the URL reveal anything about the author or source? examples: .com .edu .gov .org .net

## Accuracy

The Reliability, Truthfulness, and Correctness of the content

- Where does the information come from?
- Does evidence support the information?
- Has the information been reviewed or refereed?
- Can you verify any of the information in another source or from personal knowledge?
- Does the language or tone seem unbiased and free of emotion?
- Are there spelling, grammar, or typographical errors?

## Purpose

The reason the information exists.

- What is the purpose of the information? Is it to inform, teach, sell, entertain, or persuade?
- Do the authors/sponsors make their intentions or purpose clear?
- Is the information fact, opinion, or propaganda?
- Does the point of view appear objective and impartial?
- Are there political, ideological, cultural, religious, institutional, or personal biases?

# SWOT Analysis

SWOT stands for strengths, weaknesses, opportunities, and threats. A SWOT method of analysis is a standard test to validate your market research and analyze your competitors. On the next page, you will do a SWOT analysis of your idea.

## Strengths

In what area is your organization one step ahead of another?

_____

_____

_____

_____

_____

What is it that you can do better than anyone else?

_____

_____

_____

_____

_____

What one of a kind or lowest-cost assets can you draw upon that others can't

_____

_____

_____

_____

_____

What do individuals in the same marketplace with you observe as your source of strength?

_____

_____

_____

_____

_____

What is it about you or your business that helps your business in "getting the sale" "?

_____
_____
_____
_____
_____

## Weaknesses

How can you improve?

_____
_____
_____
_____
_____

What do you have to avoid?

_____
_____
_____
_____
_____

What do people in the marketplace see as your weaknesses?

_____
_____
_____
_____
_____

What factors do you believe makes you lose sales?

_____
_____
_____

_____

_____

## Opportunities

What other great opportunity can you point out?

_____

_____

_____

_____

What interesting trends do you have knowledge of?

_____

_____

_____

_____

## Threats

What are the obstacles facing you or your business in terms of sales, growth, or experience?

_____

_____

_____

_____

What do you think are the plans and strategy of your competitors?

_____

_____

_____

_____

Do you offer a quality product?

_____

_____

_____

_____

_____

Are the changes in technology affecting your position negatively?

_____

_____

_____

_____

_____

Do you have awful debts or income issues?

_____

_____

_____

_____

_____

Do you think that any of your weaknesses could hinder your business growth?

_____

_____

_____

_____

_____

## Additional Information

Do remember that research is a large area of study and you will find a number of ways to approach it. What we have highlighted above is just the tip of the iceberg. Spend time understanding what research can do for you. The importance of research will be dependent on your business idea and its complexity. To read a bit more about how research can help your business visit the following sites:

- https://www.entrepreneur.com/article/175276
- https://www.entrepreneur.com/article/217345
- https://www.entrepreneur.com/article/241080
- https://www.entrepreneur.com/article/43024
- http://smallbusinessbc.ca/article/how-research-your-market/
- https://www.wikihow.com/Conduct-Market-Research

This is just a starter and a lot more well-structured course content is available online for you to explore.

# 4 VALIDATING YOUR IDEA
The foundation – building the backbone of your business

Most people will tell you that every idea worth building a business around has already been taken and that there is way too much competition in the market for someone new to start and make some profit while doing so. While they are not necessarily wrong, they are not right. This competition, of course, makes it a fair gamble to start a business, but it does not reduce new business success possibilities to zero. What we must do is first set up a mechanism to test the business idea in our controlled environment before going all out to make it happen in the real world. Now the question that one must grapple with is as follows: Can we validate a business idea without spending a fortune in setting it up, or can we do it in a reasonable time frame so that we can capitalize on the opportunity window? The answer most definitely is YES. We will spend this chapter detailing the ways of validating a business idea before we start our business.

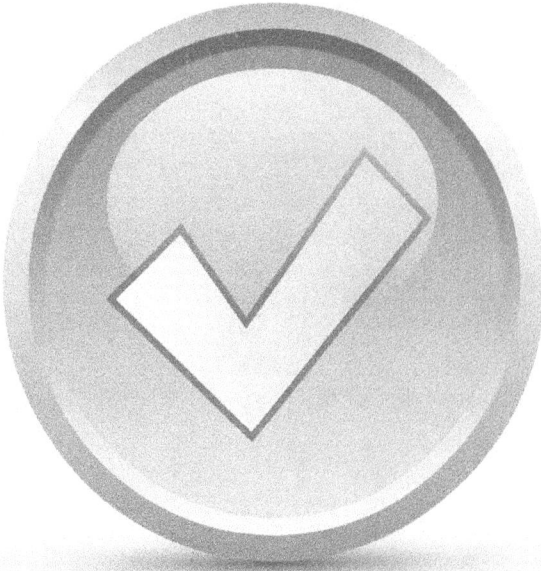

*Figure 12: Make sure you have validated your idea before continuing!*

## Thinking Realistically

Before we continue down this path, we need to think of many of the questions that will be very heavy and forward focused that can guide you on determining if this is precisely what you want?

Do I still have a personal interest in this idea?

Yes          No

What are my ballpark investment costs like?

Yes          No

Do I have the capital to invest in this idea?

Yes          No

Are there better ideas I am overlooking?

Yes          No

Would I be comfortable sticking with and growing this business?

Yes          No

Do I see myself doing this in the next 10, 20, or 30 years?

Yes          No

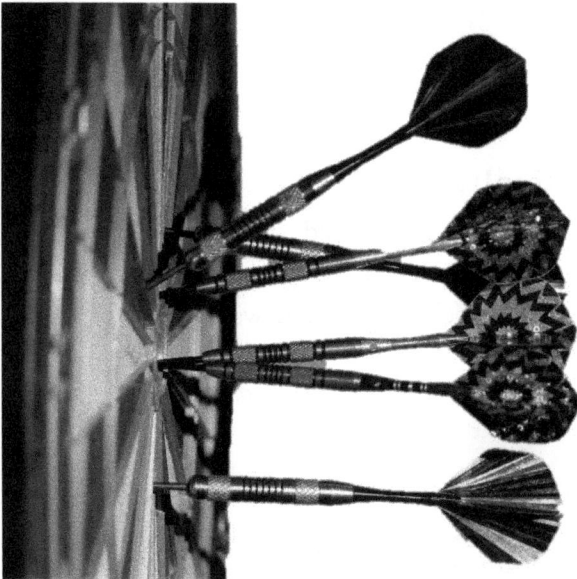

*Figure 13: Only do things you can hit the bull's eye on!*

## Quantifying your target market

Making sure you know **precisely** who is in your target market proves essential to verify your idea. From the last chapter, we were able to narrow this down. Keep this information central. This target market will now be guiding every business refinement detail we will be changing.

## Play the game to your strengths and Outsource Your Weaknesses

Building a business will demand much effort. To be successful, we must focus on areas we are good at or else, we will be caught with things we do not know how to do well and make mistakes that may be devastating. It is just like how a baker would hire an accountant. The baker is good at banking—not accounting. By focusing on your own strengths, you can do what *you* do best, not stressing over semantics that do not help your bottom line.

Furthermore, People who only do what makes them happy will be happier! We want to enjoy our new online eVenture, right!

How can I accentuate my strengths:

_____

_____

_____

_____

_____

_____

How can I bury my weaknesses:

_____

_____

_____

_____

_____

_____

*Figure 14: Testing things in small scale will help you see if your idea has potential!*

## Test Your Idea in a controlled small scale

To gauge initial interest in your idea, have a casual conversation with a few people in your target market. You do not need anything super official looking yet, but just talking to people about whether an idea would be a good fit for you and whether they think the idea would be viable. The objective of this conversation is to ensure we are building a product/service they require.

You can start with texting, emailing, and messaging friends, former co-workers, and acquaintances. A short time of about a week will have a fair number of responses for being part of your early feedback group.

You can start building your feedback group right now by working your way down this list:

- Friends & family
- Co-workers
- Former co-workers or collogues
- Other professionals, you have worked with
- Classmates or former classmates from school
- Teachers or professors you have had
- Other members of clubs, societies, groups or meetup networks you're in
- Scroll through your recent text messages. Browse through your last couple hundred personal emails. Head to your Facebook friend list, LinkedIn connection list and check out your Twitter followers.

It is always prudent to start with people you know, people who have an active interest in what you are building. Then, once you have a set of people who have expressed interest in your work, ask them to reach out to their contact circles for anyone who may be interested in or excited about what you are building

People in my early feedback group:

- _____
- _____
- _____
- _____
- _____
- _____
- _____
- _____

- _____
- _____

With this done, there are groups and platforms online that can be tapped into for a larger set of potential customers or feedback group members to give you feedback on what you are building

Engage with some standalone Online Communities:

- AMEX Open Forum for Small Business Owners
- Angel.co
- Inbound.org
- GrowthHackers
- HackerNews
- Quora
- ProductHunt
- Amazon Reviews
- Facebook Groups (Topical)

It is best if you can find topically relevant groups to join--that is where you'll know without a doubt that your target audience already exists.

## Facebook Groups

If you aren't able to find many topical Facebook Groups with a decent number of members (think 5,000+), you can still take to building a feedback community by activating members of entrepreneurial Facebook Groups where members are already conditioned to helping each other with projects like this. Start with these:

- Freedom Hackers Mastermind
- The Smart Passive Income Community
- The Joyful Entrepreneur
- Heart-centered, soul-driven entrepreneurs
- Coaches, Authors, Entrepreneurs
- Women's Entrepreneur Network (Women only!)
- Super Hero Entrepreneurs
- LinkedIn Groups (Entrepreneurial)
  - On Startups
  - Future Trends
  - I Heart Startups
  - Entrepreneur's Network
  - Band of Entrepreneurs
- Reddit Sub-Reddits
  - r/SideProject
  - r/Entrepreneur
  - r/Startups
  - r/BusinessHub
  - r/MutualCollaboration

How am I going to verify my idea online?

_____

_____

_____

_____

When you post online, remember that when you ask something of someone, they hope to get something in return, whether that would be an article about something that pertains to them or a freebie, it would be beneficial to provide something of value to people before you ask them for help online.

Another great way to gauge some of the issues that current solutions to problems have is by reading reviews online of similar products and services. You can see if there are any hints about how you can provide a superior service from the rant of some disgruntled customer. It may be beneficial to understand what their issues were with the previous product or service and develop one that is better.

*Figure 15: Talking directly with potential customers can give you useful ideas on how to better differentiate your product or fill their need better*

## Talk with your users

A business can only be built based on a solution or product that is needed by the target audience. As I seem to be mentioning more and more in this book, it is absolutely essential to talk to people and verify the need before you risk your time and effort on

During the challenge described by Ryan Robinson, a few of his conversations with the early feedback members naturally transitioned into brainstorming sessions in which the audience started telling him what they wanted. This is fantastic because you are getting dictated exactly what the market wants. Make sure when you go to talk with users, take notes, but not to the point where it becomes detracting from the conversation. Active listening is essential rather than staring when someone is trying to tell you something they want in a product.

When you work with people and listen to what they have today, your conversation will naturally evolve into them telling you what a pain point in their lives is or something that is not satisfied by traditional market offerings is. While you can have these conversations online and not in person, there is nothing like meeting your early feedback group in person and talking to them directly`. You can gauge emotion and the authenticity of their conversation. Additionally, it makes you seem more personal by coming to see them, rather than asking them to do something for you online.

There are many great questions to ask your target market, so take the time to fill some of these out and learn what you want out of your early feedback group.

- What do you want to learn from talking to your early feedback group?
- What are you currently using?
- What do you like about the current solution?
- What do you not like about the current solution?
- Is there anything you would add to the current solution?
- Is there anything holding you back from other solutions on the market?
- Would you be willing to pay for a solution that does everything you have outlined?

People I am going to talk to:

  1. _____

  2. _____

  3. _____

  4. _____

  5. _____

  6. _____

  7. _____

  8. _____

  9. _____

10. _____

Questions I am going to ask:

  1. _____
     _____

  2. _____
     _____

  3. _____
     _____

  4. _____
     _____

  5. _____
     _____

  6. _____
     _____

  7. _____
     _____

  8. _____
     _____

  9. _____
     _____

10. _____
     _____

# The Purpose of Active Listening

Listening is one of the most common and essential things that we do. Recent research on work behavior suggests that we spend approximately 9% of our time writing, 16% of our time reading, 30% of our time talking, and 45% of our time listening.

Listening is a fundamental part of the communication process. Regardless of the type of job you do or the industry in which you work, it is good to understand the listening process, have an awareness of barriers to listening effectively, and learn how to listen actively.

## Listening as a process

Hearing and listening are not the same thing. Hearing is just the first of three stages in the listening process, all of which are fairly obvious but still worth remembering.

- Hearing: Simply the process of sound waves being transformed by our brains into impulses.
- Attention: This is important so that we can hear what is being said to us, but often difficult due to distractions such as noise intrusion or internal distractions such as thinking about something else rather than what is being said.
- Understanding: This is the most crucial aspect of the process on several levels. As well as understanding what is being said, we need to try to understand the context of the message and understand the significance of any verbal or non-verbal clues from the speaker. Having a degree of background knowledge regarding the speaker or the subject is also helpful.

## Barriers to listening

In most situations, there are many obstacles that can stop us from listening effectively. It is essential to appreciate what these obstacles are and how to overcome each of them. There are four types of barriers to listening:

-   Psychological barriers, including prejudice, apathy, or fear on the part of the listener. For example, someone working in marketing or production may not be as interested in a presentation on annual financial results as an accountant or sales director, given that it may not directly impact on their day to day activities.
-   Physical barriers, including disability, fatigue, or poor health on the part of the listener. For example, trying to listen to a speaker for long periods while you are suffering from a heavy cold is a somewhat tricky thing to do.
-   Environmental barriers, including distracting noises, uncomfortable or poorly positioned seating, or an unsuitable climate such as an overheated, stuffy meeting room.
-   Expectation barriers, such as anticipating a mundane or boring presentation, expecting to receive bad news, or being spoken to in confusing jargon.

In a work or educational situation, you can undoubtedly address tangible barriers such as environmental factors or physical obstacles. Dealing with internal obstacles can be more difficult, but a lot of this can be achieved through thorough preparation before any meetings or group sessions.

## Active listening

To understand the concept and value of active listening, it is worth considering it as one of three different types of listening.

-   Competitive listening: You will see this most often in negotiation situations, or when politicians are debating with each other. The person being spoken to is more interested in getting their point of view across when the other person stops talking, rather than acknowledging what they have just heard. Alternatively, they are distracted by thinking about their argument or point of view rather than listening properly.

- Passive or attentive listening: This is always a danger in lecture-style presentation sessions. An audience will pay attention to the slides and listen carefully to the speaker, but there is no real opportunity to interact. This means that the speaker may not know how well their message is being understood.

- Active listening: This is the best way to listen for and understand the real message in what people are saying. It involves taking the next step from just listening attentively, by looking to show apparent interest in what the speaker is saying, and by trying to interact with them. As a business owner developing a new product, you need to try to use active listening yourself, and provide opportunities for colleagues, customers and leads to use active listening techniques as well. This is of particular importance when involved in informal conversations like our initial feedback session.

In terms of outlining the techniques which can be used for active listening, it is useful to think back to the three primary stages of the listening process – hearing, attention, and understanding.

## Hearing and attention

- First and hopefully obviously, stop talking.
- Try to eliminate as many distractions as possible, both external and internal.
- Try to control your non-verbal signals to the person speaking. This could mean paying attention to your physical stance, your body movements, eye contact with the speaker, and encouraging motions such as nodding or smiling.

## Understanding

- Make sure that you understand the purpose of the speaker and also be aware of what you want from the conversation.
- It also helps to take notes, but try to focus on writing down keywords and phrases that will jog your memory later, rather than trying to write down everything that is being said in the act of dictation.
- If possible, try to ask questions. You can use the notes you have written to remind you of points that need clarification. Try not to interrupt, though!
- Finally, try to use the technique of reflecting what the speaker says to you.

## Reflecting

This is a technique used extensively by people involved in consultative selling, but it is also a handy tool for anyone involved in business, education, training, or voluntary work. Communication can be broken down into three levels – facts, thoughts (or beliefs), and feelings (or emotions). Reflecting works on all three levels.

- Repeat the facts that you think the speaker has given you. This repeating is sometimes referred to as 'parroting.' If you are right, you know that you are getting the essential elements of what the speaker is telling you. If you have made any mistakes, this gives you both an opportunity to get back on to the same page.
- Also, share the thoughts or beliefs that you have heard, and try to convey the underlying feelings or emotions which you believe are involved. For example, the speaker may be very upset and wants you to display empathy or sympathy with their situation. It is this reflection of thoughts and feelings which distinguishes reflecting from just parroting back to the

speaker, which might get a bit tedious and annoying for all concerned.

Active listening is a handy tool when coaching or mentoring. It can also be used during feedback sessions and through the growth of our business to gain better feedback.

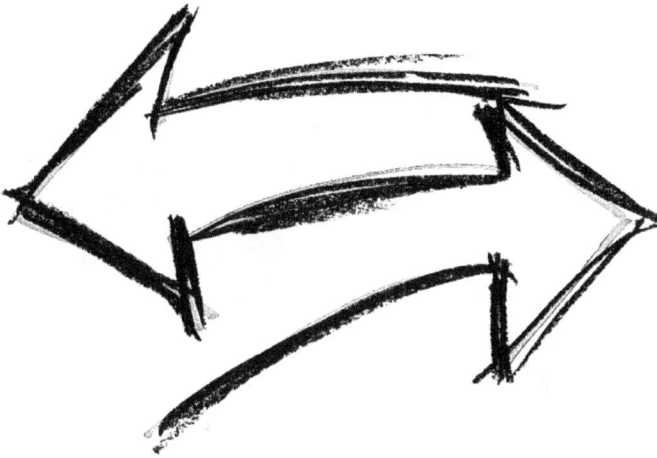

*Figure 16: What sets you apart?*

## Refine your Differentiator

With several detailed discussions with your target audience and with many of your questions answered, it is time to build a small but significant list of people who are interested in getting updates on your upcoming solution.

It is now time to expand on the plan that was created earlier. Add some more insights from the feedback you have a gathering from your conversations with the people in your community. All to develop a certain advantage that will make your solution under development uniquely valuable to your audience.

A competitive advantage is defined as the unique advantage that allows you as a business to generate higher sales or margins and or acquire and retain more customers than competitors. In short, it is what makes your business, *your* business.

From gaining insight from talking with your target market, you can now look to refine the business and the idea to fit their needs better. By improving the differentiator or competitive advantage, you can make yourself stand out in the market.

Your competitive advantage can come in many different forms, including:

- Your cost structures
- Product offering
- Distribution network
- Customer support
- Your skillset
- Your experience
- Industry knowledge
- Strategic relationships
- A powerful personal brand
- The broad and engaged audience you have built

The strength of your competitive advantage will significantly affect your early results in validating your idea.

To land on the competitive advantage or advantages for your idea, start by carefully reading and interpreting all of the feedback emails, conversation notes, and ideas you've recorded from your target audience conversations so far. Look for similarities, things that stick out, trends, surprising insights, and particularly exciting ideas that catch your eye. Write them down and narrow down the ones you think you could handle and incorporate into the final product. Remember to think like an entrepreneur—notice the almighty dollar and how the different differentiators will take time to develop and produce.

I invite you to detail your competitive advantage below, more detail now can save you a headache later!

My Competitive Advantage:

_____

_____

_____

_____

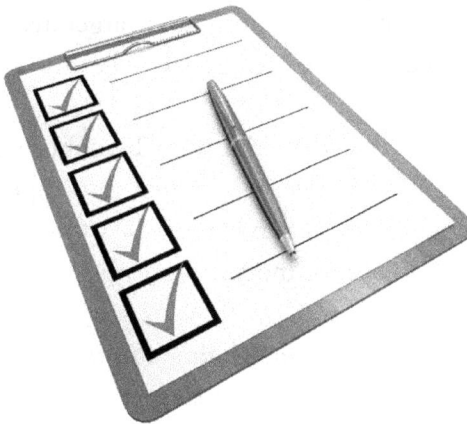

*Figure 17: Verifying your idea now has its benefits!*

# Forecasting

Taking the time now to do some quick forecasting of your expected expenses and revenue, you can roughly see what the anticipated earnings from your venture can be. In business, the monetary aspect of a venture is one of the most important parts of determining whether a company is successful or not. By doing this now, we can eliminate ideas that are not commercially viable.

When estimating revenue, take a moderate approach.

One thing I notice that people fall into is, "If there are 36 million Americans in my target market and we get 2% of those to buy our product/service at X dollars, then we will have 36,000,000 × X dollars of revenue!" Do not do this. This is flawed. You will not be able to get to this market when opening.

When I estimate revenue potential, I look at the target market within the geographic area to which I want to sell, multiply the number of people by 5%, and then assume an average growth of 4% revenue. I feel this is an incredibly modest number and helps me at least determine the amount of risk with an idea. This small estimation can give you a rough guesstimate of the money available to you. I always like to take a reserved approach on estimations such as this one, because there is no telling how much your target market will purchase the product. People can make choices for themselves.

Now you may think: 'I have no clue what I would charge for this!' That is entirely understandable. Take a look at competitor offerings and pick a number somewhere in the middle of those that you feel would be adequate to use for modeling purposes.

Below, I will guide you through creating a very basic profit and loss statement to see if there is the potential for profitability for the

Sources of Income (use as many as needed):

- _____
- _____
- _____
- _____
- _____

Revenue Year 1: (Estimated competitor monthly revenue × 12):

_____

Revenue Year 2: (Year 1 Revenue × 4%):

_____

Revenue Year 3: (Year 1 Revenue × 4%):

_____

Below, I am going to address some common expenses that entrepreneurs usually face when they startup

Initial Costs (Stuff you only Buy Once)
- Desk: _____
- Computer: _____
- Chair: _____
- Desk Lamp: _____
- Development Costs: _____
- Other: _____

Yearly Costs (Things you purchase once a year)
- Business Cards: _____
- Domain Name: _____
- Office Supplies: _____

Monthly Costs (Things you purchase each month)
- Web Hosting: _____
- Accountant Services: _____
- Billing System: _____
- SaaS Software: _____
- Marketing Materials: _____
- Software Maintenance Costs: _____

Total Expenses Year 1: (onetime purchases + yearly purchases + 12 × monthly purchases): _____

Total Expenses Year 2: (yearly purchases + 12 × monthly purchases):

_____

Total Expenses Year 3: (yearly purchases + 12 × monthly purchases):

_____

# 3 Year Expected P/L

Now that we have the necessary information we need, we can go ahead and fill in this table corresponding to the correct values. Once you fill in the revenue and expenses, the profit or loss can be calculated by subtracting the expenses from the revenue. If the expenses are larger than the revenues, you will have a net loss.

|  | Year 1 | Year 2 | Year 3 |
|---|---|---|---|
| Revenue | | | |
| Expenses | | | |
| Profit (Loss) | | | |

Now that we have the table filled in, we can see the total profit of the venture over the first three years. This value can be attained by adding the bottom row of the table.

Total three-year profit or loss of my potential venture:

_____

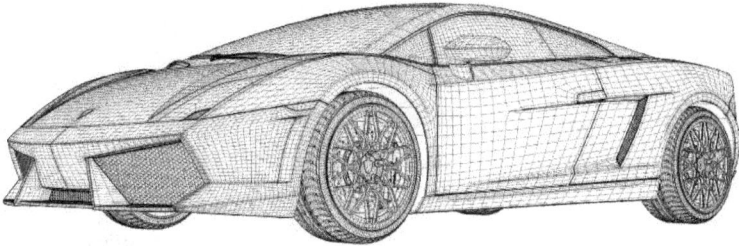

*Figure 18: Building a prototype is a great way to show target customers your product*

# Prototype your MMVP

Up until now, we really have not had anything to 'show' for our idea—nothing physical that someone can see or interact with to get the big picture. At this point, I feel it is essential to get the ball rolling on generating a Micro Minimum Viable Product, or MMVP for short. In the business world, they toss around the term Minimum Viable Product, meaning the base level product that a consumer wants. In this example, I take a pre-step to get there. This prototype is a very, *very* crude initial attempt to design something, whether that be an interface, process, screen, or physical product that someone wants in the way that is easiest for you. It doesn't need to be working at all, and shouldn't be for that matter at this stage. You are merely initially user testing your idea to make sure you are on the right track.

Instead of stopping here to invest weeks, months, or years into building your course, writing your book, developing an app or creating a website to highlight your freelance skills, we still want to make sure there's a paying demand for what you plan on building before you go out and build it. Why waste the effort!

This is where building a proof of concept prototype, or my pseudo-

Micro Minimum Viable Product comes into play. This prototype is a simple visual representation of the product you hope to make one day.

Proof of concept designs are supposed to do one thing: verify that your solution solves the problem you have identified in a commercializable way. Once you have a clearer picture of what your specific product or offering is going to be, through this idea validation process, it's time to set a goal for what you want your proof of concept to achieve.

There is no way to gauge the success of a specific prototype, but I see getting a proof of concept goal of generating a particular amount of revenue from a predefined number of paying customers as a valid metric for what we want to do. Since the service or product you develop is in the initial stages of development, it may be hard to tell this at this stage, but generally, when someone is introduced to something for the first time, they have a kind of gut reaction that will tell you if they like the product or not.

Here are some common goals that come out of creating a proof of concept:

- People rating the product 5 or higher on a survey out of 10
- Determining that the product saves a user 30 minutes in their daily life
- Setting a time for a user to complete a task in your prototype and reaching that metric

Proof of concepts can come in many forms. Some of the most common ways of creating a proof of concept are:

- Google Doc

- Explainer video
- Hand-built prototype
- Simple product sales page or website
- Rough demonstration of your software solution
- Paper screen wireframes

The proof of concept will give you the confidence needed to go further, and it will establish that there will be customers for the product you finally bring to the market.

I invite you to write down how you can effectively build a proof of concept.

My proof of concept action plan:

_____

_____

_____

_____

_____

*Figure 19: Getting preorders can help you launch with a bang!*

# Gauge Genuine Interest

Now we move onto the actual meat and potatoes of this entire process. Determining who wants to cough up the cold hard cash for your idea.

Gauging genuine interest is always the hardest part of the entire process. Now is the time when people have to invest in you, your idea, and trust that you can provide for them. This process can include setting up a crowdfunding page like Kickstarter to help get your concept preordered and funded or, in another way, get verbal commitments from users that they would be willing to give you a chance.

As for pricing your services, do not worry about this too much right now. These people are risking a lot by trusting you when they have not even really seen the end result of your hard work. Make sure you are fair but not overconfident in pricing. As you scale up and get entirely going, feel free to be as confident as you want because of your preexisting track record. I always find it helpful to create pricing based on current market offerings and competitors.

To get this set up correctly, we need to develop a mock launch plan:

Version Offered: _____
Introductory Pricing: _____
Contacts I will talk to:

    1. _____

    2. _____

    3. _____

    4. _____

    5. _____

How will I go about selling the product?

_____

_____

_____

_____

_____

*Figure 20: Never stop tweaking!*

# Iterative Cycles – Keep on Tweaking!

One of the things that they would never stop shoving down my throat at Purdue in my STEM education is to design, test, built, test, iterate, design, test, build, test…. And so on. This endless cycle of designing, testing, building, and iterating was essential to not only creating and adding new features to a product or service but can also be interpreted to our business as well… Or an author who keeps trying to rewrite a book before putting it out. Making sure we not only stay current but always tweak what we do to ensure that people are satisfied and the client is happy is essential to sustained business.

If you successfully validate your idea, you have more affirmation that you are going to be providing something that the market needs for and is willing to pay for! If you feel that the market has not proven what you wanted it to, do not give up!

If you have felt that through this process, you have been unable to validate your idea sufficiently, take a step back, and see if this is truly an idea worth pursuing. If it is not, feel free to shelve it and start over! That is all part of the process.

Here are some of the most common reasons validation tests fail:
- Pitching to the wrong audience
- Not getting in front of a broad enough audience
- Not creating enough perceived value in your proof of concept
- Not incorporating or highlighting the right value propositions
- Pricing the pre-order of your solution above what your audience will pay
- Existing solutions on the market are already "good enough."

*Figure 21: Wait, this is not an actual elevator pitch!*

## Creating an Elevator Pitch

In my Entrepreneurship classes, I have been taught over and over again to refine your elevator pitch. I have deliberately not mentioned it until now to make sure that I can cover how to prepare a great one in detail.

An elevator pitch, or speech, is a short verbal snippet that clearly and memorably introduces you or your idea or company. It highlights your uniqueness and focuses on the benefits you provide.

Imagine: you step onto an elevator, and a lone occupant is waiting to travel with you to another floor.

You are together for less than a minute, but long enough to make polite conversation.

What you do not know is that this person is your ideal client. They have a problem you can solve.

They cut through the awkward silence and say, "I see you're attending the networking event as well. What do you do?"

Here it is! Your chance to make an impression and secure a new client.

After a short stammer, you answer with, "I'm an entrepreneur. I hold a degree in entrepreneurship and have been running my own home-based business for ten years."

With only a few seconds left, the elevator doors open. They politely respond with a smile, then steps off the elevator, gone forever.

After you finish banging your head against the button panel, you realize you not only blew it, but you now have an indentation of the twenty-first-floor button on your forehead.

What if instead, you had answered with:

"I help entrepreneurs get more clients than they know what to do with and triple their profits in six months."

If she were your target client, do you think the second response would have sparked her interest and kept her on that elevator a little bit longer?

We all ask ourselves, "What's in it for me?" when engaged in any communication, whether written or spoken.

You want to take something of value from a conversation, learn something new, create a certain feeling, or receive information that will help you solve a problem or meet a need.

If you spend the first 30 seconds labeling yourself and listing your credentials, or going into a technical spiel of your product or service, you will be met with nothing more than a big fat yawn, a glazed-over look or even worse, "Excuse me, I have to make a call" and a quick exit.

Take the time to develop a benefit-rich, passionate elevator speech that will engage your listeners to want to hear more.

Write down a list of benefits your clients/customers receive from working with you or buying from you and use those words and phrases in your benefit statement.

There is no need to label yourself. Labels do not provide the benefits the listener is looking for.

Once you have your elevator speech developed, practice it over and over until it is as natural as stating your name. You will be able to use it at networking events, in a telephone conversation, when leaving voice mail messages, in any written communication, and yes, especially in the elevator!

## The Extended Elevator Pitch

While a literal elevator pitch is useful, there comes the point where you may need to talk a little bit more about some of the benefits of your business; Some conversations may not be able to fit in the small confines of an elevator. I am coining this the extended elevator pitch, extending the little time in a lift to a much better-prepared presentation about your business idea.

An extended elevator pitch should be able to be condensed into a single-page presentation, short enough to be memorized, or read easily within a few minutes—that's how it got its name, it's a pitch that's short enough to be presented during the course of an elevator ride. The elevator pitch condenses your business concept into something that can be shown in about a minute or two—primarily, the parts that matter, the very "essence" of the business.

The extended elevator pitch skips the hard-core financials and gets straight to the heart of what it is about the business that gets you excited. That is what this type of pitch is about—you do not need the proof of concept here yet, that comes in the full-length business plan and business pitch. The elevator pitch is the commercial that gets people interested.

The elevator pitch should be inspirational and creative, hitting the high points of your business concept, and should accomplish the following:
- Hit the high points of what it is you hope to do
- Summarize the problem/solution aspect of your concept
- Briefly describe the business model—how is it going to make money?
- Create excitement on the part of the reader/listener
- Describe the profit potential without having to bring out charts and graphs

- Tell why you/your company are well-positioned to accomplish your goal
- End with a call to action

The first couple of sentences are the most critical and should present your core concept. If you cannot tell what it is you want to do in two sentences or less, then you need to simplify your concept. There will be plenty of time to get into all the details later once you have captured your audience's interest.

## Interpreting the results

In terms of determining whether this validation process proves your idea is marketable, let us reflect a bit. Where have we come from the start of this process? What have I done?

What have I proven in this process?

_____

_____

_____

Looking at this, what can you make of it? Are those good things, are they bad? Do you feel like you can take this to the next level based on your initial validation?

Furthermore, if you feel as though this validation process failed, you are not alone! Wouldn't you have instead failed now with minimal time and money invested rather than a year after launch? I find validation successful if your idea failed. That means there is not enough of a market to warrant the full-time pursual of this idea. Therefore, I genuinely encourage you to reference your list of business ideas and go through my ideation process again to see if there is any other idea that sticks out to you and try the validation process again. Don't get down, there are many great ideas that can work as well! Once you found the idea that works for you, you did it!

## Additional Information

The net has several resources that will help you build a validation model. Some of them that we like are as follows:

- https://www.entrepreneur.com/article/237455
- https://www.entrepreneur.com/article/233408
- https://www.inc.com/jeff-haden/start-a-business-9-steps-to-validate-a-business-idea-while-keeping-your-full-tim.html
- https://startupbros.com/3-steps-to-validate-your-business-idea-for-free/
- https://www.entrepreneur.com/article/289297

Coming back to the 3D printed parts business we are building throughout this book; you will require a large group of people to test your idea on. Remember to include customers from different walks of life, business owners, engineers, and people just looking for custom gifts. These people will all offer a great perspective to the business as well as bring forward their own thoughts that you may have not considered. This will make for a decent group that will help validate your idea.

# 5 TALKING TO CUSTOMERS

Understanding Customers – Your Revenue Stream

The customer is central to all our efforts. For a business to be successful, we must be able to engage with the customer and get them to buy our products or services. We have done a lot of validation and research to ensure we are on a path where the product or service we are building will fulfill a gap that the customer feels in the marketplace. It is now time to start understanding the customer better. We must acknowledge that the need we are trying to fulfill is continually changing. A market is a dynamic place. Not only do the requirements of the customer change, the way a service or product is consumed also varies. It is imperative to engage with the customer and adapt to the needs if there is a change in them. A typical business idea goes through the following stages –

1) The idea is born
2) A product or service is built around the idea
3) Measure how customers respond to the product or service
4) Learn from the feedback received from the customers
5) Refine the product or service or pivot.

It is the last step that will define the continued success of our venture. Once we have feedback from a significant number of customers, we must analyze and learn from it. It is often said that one should not be in love with the product or service one offers, let go, and change to stay relevant in the market.

Eric Ries, the author of "The Lean Startup," defines a pivot as "a structured course correction designed to test a new fundamental hypothesis about the product, strategy, and engine of growth." A pivot is not a complete restart of how you do business. Instead, it is a special kind of experiment designed to test a new supposition based on facts on past results and the underlying business model. A pivot may well be the most important of serval lessons learned directly from the customer.

An effective pivot that will give rich dividends takes learning from a running business model and makes big or small adjustments. To validate quickly, you must pivot fast and not get caught in a model that will not allow you to build a business that is both scalable and repeatable.

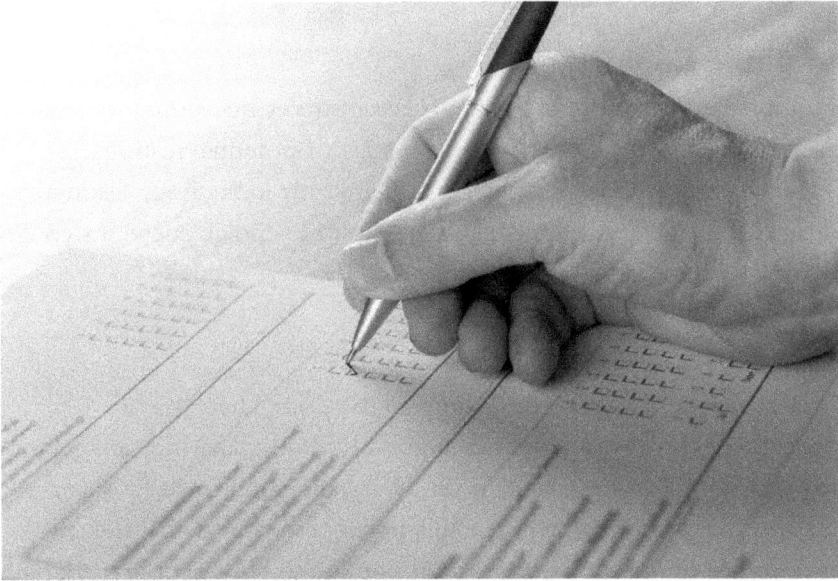

*Figure 22: Surveys are great ways to gauge interest.*

# Surveys

Surveys are a great way to get good feedback from our customers. It is free (most of the time), quick, and easy way to get massive amounts of data from your potential customers.

When you create a survey, it is essential to always start with a goal: What do you want to use this data from the survey?

My Survey's Goal:

_____

Another vital thing to keep in mind when creating your survey is that every question should have a purpose—Do not ask questions that do not directly help you achieve your goal

# Question Types

When creating a survey, it is essential to understand how the different types of questions work to get the most useful data from them.

## Multiple Choice

Multiple Choice questions are the classic survey question: you are asked a question and presented with a list of potential responses. This question type is useful when you are only looking for distinctly different answers. A lot of seemingly multiple-choice questions could work a lot better as a scale question

## Free Response

Free-response questions are left up to the user: There are no predefined choices given in this type of question, and they are great for questions that have to do with "What did you like about this feature?" or "How can you use this product in your daily life?" In these types of questions, you would not like to have people predefine the ways they would use the product; you would like to hear how each person would have a use case.

## Scale

Scale questions are relatively new, and one of my favorite types of questions to put on surveys because they yield a lot of hidden data and trends. You can ask someone about how willing they are to buy a certain product on a scale of 1 to 10. From there, you can extrapolate a total amount of data and truer numbers rather than the four choices presented by a multiple-choice question.

Incidentally, a good survey is a mix of these main question types and some other more obscure ones that you can use to capture data and accomplish the goals of your survey more effectively.

## Survey Tips

It is better to keep surveys under 15 questions, so it takes the end user only a few minutes to fill out. If it is too long, people will lose interest and not finish the survey.

Additionally, you will want to include some questions in your input that will determine if people who are taking the survey are giving good data that will help you. You can ask them if they have experience with a competitor's product or what they do as their occupation to verify that they are giving real data.

I like to send my survey to as many people I can, post it online, send it on all of my social media channels, as well as post it on some forums of potential users. These results will guide me in forming a business.

At the end of the survey, it is always important to make sure that people can sign up for your mailing list and to volunteer if they would like to get interviewed or in a focus group. In a

## Making A Survey

There are many great resources out there for you to makes surveys. There is a lot of online survey software that you can use to send surveys to people. Here are some of them:

- Google Forms
- Qualtrics
- Survey Monkey
- eSurveyCreator

Places I can send my survey:

1. _____
2. _____
3. _____
4. _____
5. _____
6. _____
7. _____
8. _____
9. _____
10. _____

Questions on my survey:

1. _____
_____
_____

2. _____
_____
_____

3. _____
_____
_____

4. _____
_____
_____

5. _____
_____
_____

6. _____
_____
_____

7. _____
_____
_____

8. _____
   _____
   _____

9. _____
   _____
   _____

10. _____
    _____
    _____

11. _____
    _____
    _____

12. _____
    _____
    _____

13. _____
    _____
    _____

14. _____
    _____
    _____

15. _____
    _____
    _____

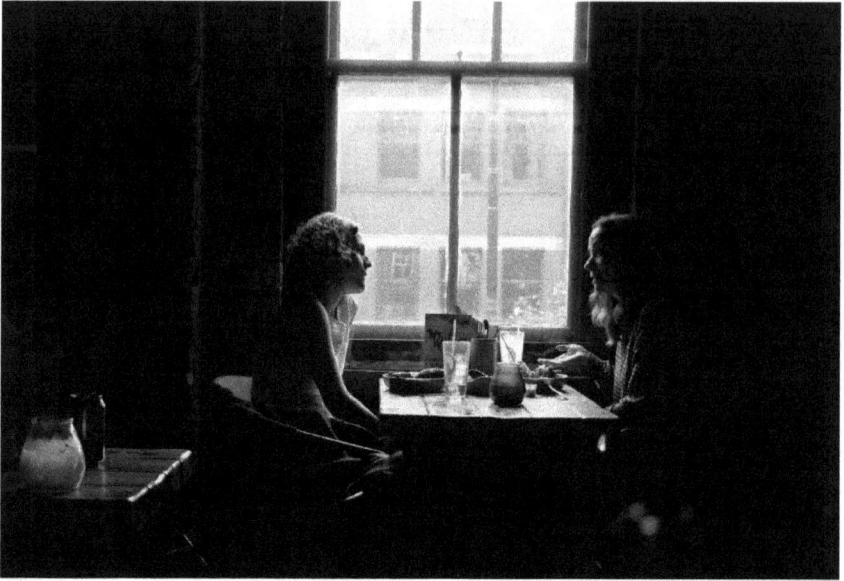

*Figure 23: Interviewing potential customers can help you refine your idea.*

# Interviews

Expanding more on the surveys, you may want to interview a few select people that would be the most representative of your ideal target customer. You can get their information from the surveys you asked people and then follow up with them. I recommend doing five interviews, so that way you can start to see trends in the way people physically react to products as well as their demeanor and other personality factors you cannot determine through a survey.

People I am going to interview:

1. _____
2. _____
3. _____
4. _____
5. _____

## **Interview Template:**

Question 1:

_____

_____

Replies:

1. _____

_____

_____

_____

2. _____

_____

_____

_____

3. _____

_____

_____

_____

4. _____

_____

_____

_____

5. _____

_____

_____

_____

Question 2:

_____

_____

Replies:

1. _____

   _____

   _____

   _____

2. _____

   _____

   _____

   _____

3. _____

   _____

   _____

   _____

4. _____

   _____

   _____

   _____

5. _____

   _____

   _____

   _____

Question 3:

_____

_____

Replies:

1. _____

   _____

   _____

   _____

2. _____

   _____

   _____

   _____

3. _____

   _____

   _____

   _____

4. _____

   _____

   _____

   _____

5. _____

   _____

   _____

   _____

Question 4:

_____

_____

Replies:

1. _____

   _____

   _____

   _____

2. _____

   _____

   _____

   _____

3. _____

   _____

   _____

   _____

4. _____

   _____

   _____

   _____

5. _____

   _____

   _____

   _____

Question 5:

_____

_____

Replies:

1. _____

   _____

   _____

   _____

2. _____

   _____

   _____

   _____

3. _____

   _____

   _____

   _____

4. _____

   _____

   _____

   _____

5. _____

   _____

   _____

   _____

*Figure 24: Groups of people in a focus group can help brainstorm new offerings as well*

# Focus Groups

Once you have a product or service set up, it may be smart to get a focus group together. In a focus group, you get a group of people together that would be representative of your target market and present them with a prototype of the service or product you have developed. A focus group takes an interview one step further–it allows people to try your product before it goes live because you want to make sure that it fully satisfies all of your customer's needs.

Additionally, focus groups can tell you a lot about the usability of an item as well. You will be able to see how they navigate your website, for example. This ability to observe real people using your service will help you get the small nuances of people using your product. That way, you will be able to make small tweaks to your product before its launch and have less headache to deal with.

Many services can do this for you on your behalf, or you can run one yourself. There are many resources online on how to run a focus group properly.

How will I implement my focus group?

_____

_____

_____

*Figure 25: Pivoting to a new idea is not always a bad thing!*

# Pivoting

Referring back to the book "The Lean Startup", Ries highlights the following pivots as possibilities:

Zoom-in pivot: A feature of the product is so useful that it becomes the whole product.

Zoom-out pivot: In the reverse situation, the whole product is included in an even larger product or platform. An example of a zoom-out pivot is Docker (the DotCloud pivot).

Product value pivot: The product benefits and promised return on investment did not catch the attention of the stakeholders. Changing the value proposition and positioning can help establish value more quickly.

Value capture pivot: The solution had value, but the revenue or business model was wrong for the customers. A new revenue model might open up new revenue opportunities.

Channel pivot: Changing the way the technology is brought to market. For example, changing from a direct sales model to a reseller go-to-market strategy.

Technology pivot: Changing the way the solution delivers results by using a completely different technology.

Customer need pivot: The problem solved was not very significant, or money was not available to buy. This may require solving a different problem with a different solution.

Customer segment pivot: The product attracts real customers, but not the ones you were initially targeting. The problem is real, but the customer group will limit your ability to scale and grow.
If you were unable to find a Product-Market fit with your current solution, the first pivot to consider should be around the solution (the product, the usage or the benefits)"

As we can see, Eric Ries knows what he is talking about with pivoting. Now I challenge you to look at the data you have been collecting and determine if you need to pivot. I also encourage you to reference this much later as you work your new business and constantly look to pivot.

Do I need to pivot? _____

If so, How?

_____

_____

_____

_____

_____

## Additional Information

Again, the net is a treasure trove of content on how to use a customer interaction to create a pivot in your business model, a few that we like are here:

- https://leanb2bbook.com/blog/how-to-pivot-a-b2b-startup/
- https://mfishbein.com/100-customer-development-interviews/
- https://www.kohactive.com/blog/pivoting-is-part-of-the-startup-process/
- https://blog.ladder.io/customer-interviews/
- https://www.startups.co/answers/1163/when-should-you-pivot-your-business-model-after-how-many-month-customer
- https://venturewell.org/customer-interviews/

The 3D printing business is extremely sensitive to how well the customers accept the final product. It is critical that we keep listening to customer feedback and to effectively use this feedback to change our approach to the business. The customers, in this case, will include engineers, customization lovers, and business owners. Understanding their comfort zone can define our success or failure. Utilizing proper interviews and focus groups will gauge how people react to the idea and further develop the project to be exactly what people need.

# 6 BUILDING YOUR MONEY MAKING MACHINE

The tools of the trade – a computer that delivers

Life on the web starts with a few basics – a computer that can do all the things you need getting done, a web hosting service, a decent uplink to the internet for you to stay connected, and the website, which will be your primary asset to build your business. The main tool for an online business will be your personal computer. The unit must be ready to take on the challenges of the business you decide to build. It is advisable to build your machine against buying one off the shelf. Since there are high volumes of pre-built units being built by PC manufacturers, they often use lower quality parts, and because of that, the machines have a shorter lifespan. I advise strongly in favor of understanding the requirement of your business and the demands it will have from the computer and then building a custom system to satisfy those needs. When you buy a prebuilt system, you lose the ability to upgrade as easily as well as design a computer that will be completely specific to your exact business needs.

To give you a simple understanding, if writing content is the venture you wish to pursue, a basic computer with a word processing software will do the trick. On the flip side, if you are a movie editor, then you will require not just large amounts of storage. You will also require a lot of good high-speed RAM, a capable processor, and a high-end graphics card. Most off the shelf devices will not be able to deliver the processing power or the graphics ability required for this kind of work. You will also require high-end software that most units do not have the capability of running efficiently unless you design a system that is specifically designed for the workload and demands of the task at hand.

Now, if you are selling 3D printed parts, then you will require a system that will be able to run computer-aided design software and have enough processing power to be able to convert the designs into 3D printer code to be read by the 3D printer. You will require minimal editing capabilities if you need to make videos showing off the service others. You will require a good web hosting service that can show your web content to the prospective and current clients with quick loading times. You also require a good website design to engage the audience with better results. We presume you have a dedicated computer for actually dispatching the 3D printing jobs to the printer once you model and 'slice' the component into 3D printer code. This text will only concentrate on the unit needed to manage and provide for your web business.

There are many strong reasons to build your PC. One of them is cost. If you require a decent performing PC, you will save if you do it yourself. The other reason to build your PC is the ease of upgrade. Your business will require you to move with the times. A self-assembled unit will give you the flexibility you require for the upgrade as and when you require it. It will not have built-in parts or proprietary assemblies that you cannot upgrade. Unfortunately, with new technological advances and thinner laptops, processors and other components have been built into one standard assembly that makes it harder to upgrade. In self-built systems, you have the ability to upgrade exactly the part you want when you want rather than having to buy a whole new motherboard, processor, and hard disk combo when you only want to upgrade the processor. You also have the option of overclocking on a custom-built system to extract some extra performance from your unit.

# PC Components

Building your own PC will require you to select components to put together into a working system. You will have to select the following six components to make sure that you build a complete, working computer.

## Case

The PC case is what holds all the internal components together in a structure. Also known as an enclosure or chassis, there many different size cases based on the size or 'form factor' of the motherboard.

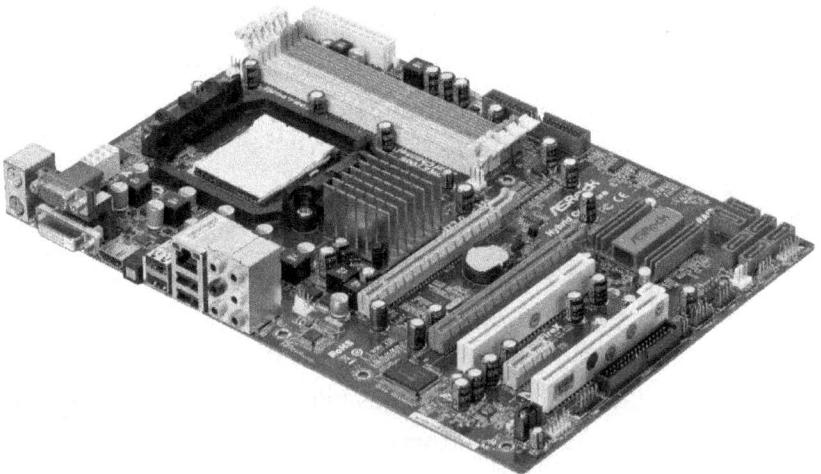

*Figure 26: A motherboard*

# Motherboard

The motherboard is the connective tissue of your PC build. Every other component will be attached to or plugged into the motherboard in some fashion. The motherboard holds the processor of the computer, the RAM, and allows you to be able to connect the hard drive storage to the computer. It also allows you to connect the display, mouse, and keyboard on the rear of the unit.

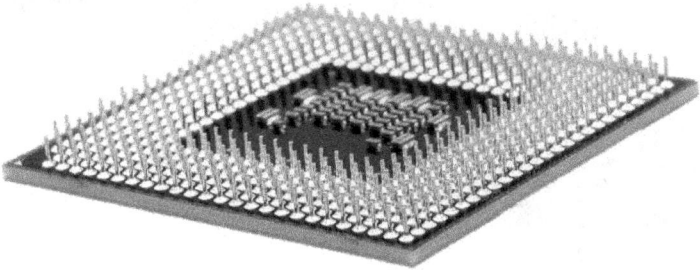

*Figure 27: A CPU*

## Processor (or CPU)

The central processing unit, or CPU, is the "brain" of your PC. This will mainly determine the speed of your computer. The CPU actually crunches the numbers and does the math that a computer is designed to do. It does the computation needed to run the programs that you and your business need to be productive. You will have to choose a CPU and a motherboard that are compatible with each other, both in terms of the manufacturer (Intel or AMD) and the CPU socket itself. Since it is essential to making the PC run at optimal speed, I usually design computers around the CPU. In today's market, many CPU models have multiple cores. Multiple cores mean that the processor can do that number of operations at the same time. For example, a 4-

core processor can do four logical processes per second. CPU Cores is not to be confused with the number of programs that a computer can run at one time; it is merely the amount of computation the processor can do at once.

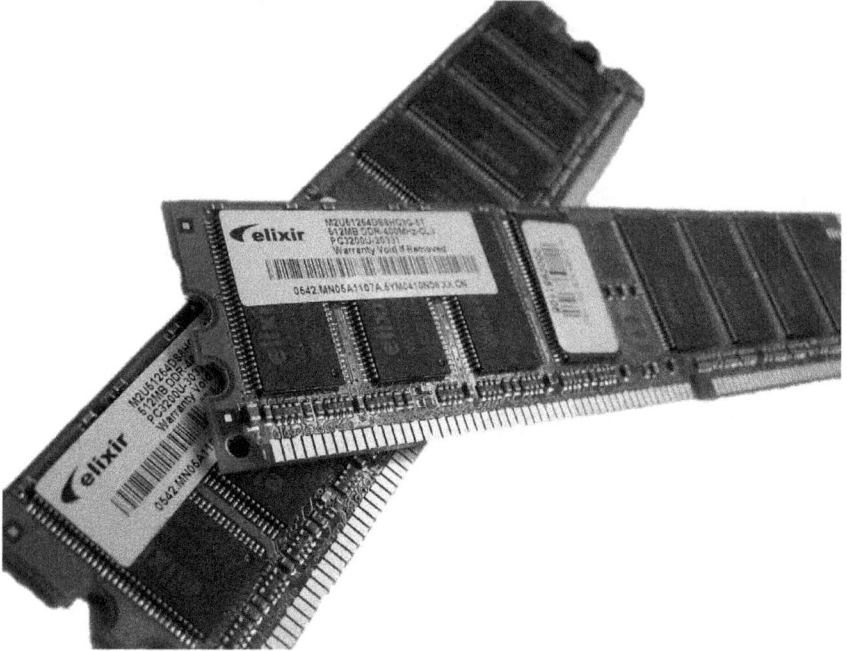

*Figure 28: RAM modules*

## Memory (or RAM)

RAM is a crucial component of your computer's operation. RAM, or Random Access Memory, is the memory that your processor can get to the quickest and provides a buffer to the programs running on your computer. You need to choose RAM that is compatible with your motherboard's RAM slots. These parts usually come in long sticks that slip into slots on the motherboard. Consult the user manual of your motherboard into finding the right size, type, and speed of memory that you need for your system. In most cases, about 8-16 GB of RAM is sufficient.

*Figure 29: A traditional hard disk drive*

## Storage

Your hard drive (HDD) or solid-state drive (SSD) is the part of the computer that holds the operating system and all your digital files. SSDs are much faster than hard drives and are highly recommended these days, though HDDs are generally larger and cheaper. This medium of storage is very large and connects to your motherboard easily. In terms of hard drives, they work by rotating silicon plates that store data. In SSDs, there are no moving parts, and thus the time to retrieve data is much quicker. It is up to you with which type of storage you want to use, but generally, a mix of both SSDs and HDDs are great for any purpose.

*Figure 30: A computer Power Supply*

## Power Supply (or PSU)

The PSU, or Power Supply Unit is a heavy little box that regulates the electricity going into your computer and provides power to everything inside your PC. The power supply will connect to the motherboard, CPU, storage, and other components as needed. People generally overlook the power supply, even though it is essential to the overall computer. Since the power supply could be compared to the blood vessels in your body, it supplies the power that your computer needs to every individual part. It is important to make sure that you have the right power rating with all of the components needed in the system. A simple google search for 'computer power supply calculator' will give you a plethora of websites where you can enter information about the parts in your computer and then calculate the power supply needed automatically.

## Cooling

One more important component will be the heat sink or the cooling system of your CPU. If you opt for a high-performance machine, a good cooling unit is critical. Some of the newer coolers use a new type of water-cooling loop enclosed in a loop. In general, though, a cooler with a bit more power than the one included with your CPU will be able to provide you with enough cooling you need for your system.

# Peripheral Components

You will have to spend some time defining the requirements around the peripherals as well. Computer peripherals include the display, keyboard, mouse, and digital input pen if needed. With graphic designing or video editing requirements, you must have a good and large display. Your monitor should be color calibratable for working on pictures and video, so the colors seen on the screen are the actual colors shown. You may also need a designer's mouse, which is a specialized mouse that gives more control and is better calibrated for design work as against the regular mouse. As a creative designer, you may opt for a "pen" for specific design requirements. The digital input pen allows you to be able to 'draw' on a pad that translated to mouse movement on the screen. If video editing is required, you will also require a decent quality speaker set as it will help get the sound effects right. Mixing sound with video is an art that requires well-coordinated eyes and ears.

The last but not the least requirement will be of a power backup or Uninterruptable Power Supply and a data backup setup. In today's world, everything can be backed up on a cloud storage solution. Choose the one that fits your requirements and the cost structure, but please put it in place. I have had hard drive failures that cost lots of money to get critical data back. I cannot stress enough how important it is to have a backup. Backing up your information in the cloud is well worth the money. The power backup will ensure two things: first, the power quality to your computer will be good, and without major fluctuation that would cause your computer to shut down prematurely, and second, it will save you much heartburn if a blackout or brownout occurs during some heavy work that you were doing. That would cause the computer to immediately power off or restart, causing you to lose all of your work. This power backup unit will prevent that and allow you to be able to save your work and safely power down your computer on the unit's battery instead of catastrophic power failure.

## Other Components

Now the keen among you should be able to see that I missed talking about some other important parts to computers, These parts aren't necessarily needed in every computer, or you could get away with the stock parts that come with some of the other main parts. Once again, this depends entirely on the designed and intended use of your system.

*Figure 31: A Graphics Card*

### Graphics Card

Most CPUs come with onboard graphics that will run daily tasks just fine. But if you plan on running intense media applications like video editing, 3D modeling, or gaming, you will want a separate graphics card that plugs into one of the PCI-Express ports on the motherboard. A video card will accelerate the rendering of the graphics that you see on the screen and will allow you to connect many monitors and outputs to your system. A graphics card is almost essential to any homebuilt PC today.

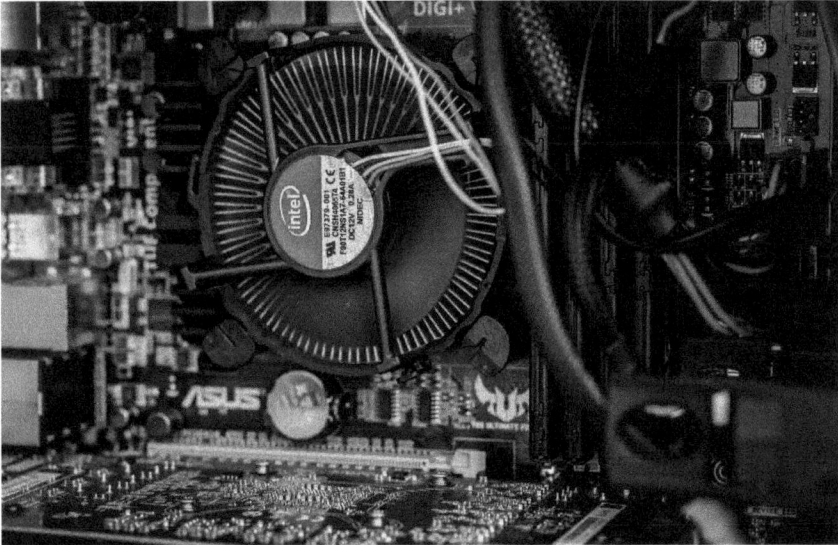

Figure 32: A CPU cooler properly mounted in a system

## CPU Cooler

All but the most expensive CPUs come with a heatsink and fan inside the box—this is essential to keep your computer from overheating. If you are planning on using your PC for high-end applications, or if you want to overclock, or squeeze more performance out of it at some point, you will want a bigger, more robust cooler. These come in air-cooled and water-cooled varieties.

*Figure 33: All the Storage!*

## Extra Storage

You can add as many hard drives or storage drives as your motherboard can handle, up to its maximum number of SATA ports. I would recommend having at least one extra drive to keep files that you do not access as often on. A good rule of thumb that I use is to make sure that the operating system and all of the programs that you frequently use are on one Solid-state drive, and the files you do not access as much or just store are on another traditional spinning hard drive.

*Figure 34: A Disk Drive*

## DVD or Blu-ray Drive

A disk drive used to be required to install an operating system, but today, most users have switched to simply loading up installation files on a USB drive. A separate disc drive is only useful if you have a lot of media still on discs that you need to access frequently. Video editing applications will require this for sure, as well as being able to deliver videos physically. Nowadays, it is not super essential to have this, but they are so cheap and useful. I do not see a reason not to have one.

*Figure 35: A traditional case fan*

## Case Fans

Most PC cases will come with one or two fans to get you started, but if you're serious about making sure that your system is always running at its peak, you will want to use fans to keep the internals of your system cool.

Additionally, you may want to get aftermarket fans that are not as loud or intrusive. Make sure that you procure fans that are the correct sizes for the mounting on your case. You can consult your case's specifications or user manual to find out the actual sizes your case needs. In addition, there are two ways a fan can point. It can let air into the case (intake) or let out air (exhaust). It is crucial to make sure that the fan direction allows for an easy flow of air through the system and over all parts that need to be cooled including the CPU, graphics card, and chips on the motherboard with heatsinks.

## Add-on Components

Thanks to PCI-E, SATA, and M2 ports on the motherboard, you

have a lot of various connectivity options to expand the usefulness of your system. Furthermore, your case may have connectors that allow you to have additional USB ports, sound jacks, or even a hard drive connector. It is always good to make sure that everything is compatible though

The only rule you must always follow is to **Double, Triple, and Quadruple Check Your Parts for Compatibility!** You can do this by plugging your components into a website like PCPartPicker.com, and it will automatically determine the power supply you need, find the best deals for you from several different stores, and cross-check compatibility for the parts.

## Individual Needs

Your specific needs for each individual component will vary based on the kind of computer you want to build and your budget, as well as your anticipated use case. You can select the right parts by referencing the internet, your motherboard's reference manual, or PC Part Picker. It is essential to remember to choose parts that work with each other. Before you purchase anything, it is essential to read the next few sections and understand what the compatibility constraints are.

**Processor:** Your processor needs to have the same socket type as that of your motherboard and be allowed on the motherboard's allowed processors list. You can usually find this information in the reference manual of the motherboard I usually plan my systems around the CPU I wish to use, and then find a motherboard that has all of the necessary features I am looking for.

**Motherboard:** Your motherboard needs to have the correct socket to accept the CPU. You can find the socket type of the processor in the CPU specifications. Additionally, this will be the board to which everything else plugs into. You will need to select RAM that has the correct socket and speed for the CPU and motherboard. Another thing to keep a note of is that the motherboard is what allows you to have the built-in features like USB C or USB ports that you wish to have in the final build. Make sure you take your time and select a motherboard that has all of the features that you desire in your computer.

**RAM:** As noted above, your RAM needs to match the type, speed, and type of slots on the motherboard (DDR3 or DDR4). You can consult your motherboard's user manual to find the correct speed, size, and type of memory.

**Storage:** Your storage needs to be able to fit inside your case in the correct storage bays and size as well as have the correct type of connection to your motherboard. Most drives that are not special use a SATA or M.2 connector. Most standard motherboards now have these connectors built into them. Making sure that you select the correct size, making sure the power connector is one that your power supply has on it, and the correct interface is enough to make sure the parts are compatible with each other.

**Case:** Your case needs to fit everything in it. Your case is the outer look of the system as well. I encourage you to take the notion of function over looks. I do realize that many cases look cool out there but may not allow you to do everything you want with it. I encourage you to make sure that you take advantage of all of the drive bays, connectors, front panel ports, and expansion bays you can in a case to make sure this is a part that you will be able to use in the future. You can find the sizes of the motherboard in the specifications for the motherboard. Make sure the form factor fits your motherboard!

**Graphics card:** As for your graphics card, your motherboard needs to support the correct PCIe bus to be able to connect your graphics card to, and you need to make sure that the power demands of the card can also be satisfied as well by your PSU. Furthermore, your graphics card needs to fit the size of your case and needs the right connector on your power supply. Generally, the biggest concern with finding a graphics card is making sure your power supply can handle it.

**CPU cooler:** Your cooler needs to be able to fit your CPU socket and be slim enough to fit inside of the case. In the case of water cooling, you also need to make sure there is enough space to mount a radiator as well as the runs of coolant hose.

**Power supply:** Your power supply needs the right overall electrical capacity for your build, as well as needs the correct number of pins on motherboard and CPU rail. Additionally, you will want to make sure that the power supply you choose has all of the necessary plugins for the drives, graphics card, and the various add-ins that you choose to add to the system.

Making sure all of the parts are compatible may seem daunting but again, a site like PCPartPicker.com can do most of the matching and advice for you—then you can double-check the specifications sheets and make sure everything matches up.

The internet is full of content on how to build your computer. We encourage you to explore as much as you can. We have done some basic research to help you with the starting points, do visit the following site for starters:

- http://www.tomshardware.com/forum/355046-31-guide-choosing-computer-parts
- https://www.digitaltrends.com/computing/pc-build-guide/
- https://www.howtogeek.com/howto/the-geek-blog/building-a-new-computer-part-1-choosing-hardware/

- http://www.techradar.com/news/computing-components/how-to-build-the-best-pc-for-your-needs-1027825
- http://ccm.net/faq/6731-building-a-new-pc-how-to-choose-the-right-hardware
- https://lifehacker.com/5840963/the-best-pcs-you-can-build-for-600-and-1200
- http://www.tomshardware.com/reviews/build-your-own-pc,2601-7.html

We would like to attract your attention to one more component of your work-life – the desk and chair you use for work. Invest time and energy in choosing the best you can get unless you have one that works well now. Long hours on your desk require many comforts, and a good investment here will give you returns over a long time. A comfy chair that will get many many hours of use will be a very worthwhile investment here.

Some tips for building the PC for our extended example of the 3D printing business: This is a business machine we want for modeling components, and to creating and maintaining the code our website that sells parts for the custom gift industry utilizes. Now the printer is a heavy-duty application but, the PC will be much faster than the printer can ever be. So, the PC needs to ensure it can send the print instructions to the printer and then wait for the output to happen. Additionally, you will need to run a word processor, code editor, spreadsheet application, and a program to access the internet. In terms of modeling, most CAD software will run better on a computer with a faster processor and a good graphics card, but in general, you will be able to get away with a mid-range PC. It is also important to note that you should look at the recommended hardware requirements to make sure that the computer you are designing will be powerful enough to run the software you will be using daily.

# PC Types

In our example business, the capabilities of the PC will be tested when generating CAD designs. Given that we are selling custom-made specialty parts for use with custom machines, we will have to have several videos that will explain how our work benefits the patient and how creative people can utilize their services to help their patients. Creating these videos and mixing them with voice and text is an extensive computing activity, and we must have a PC that can do this well. By investing in such a PC, we will save on the time required to create the videos and content needed to keep the business running.

Generally, we can Classify PCs into broad categories as follows:
A. **The Everyday Machine** – Low in specs, low in storage, single or dual-core processor, low RAM, no graphics. This machine is perfect for things that anyone would normally do—surf the web, write documents.
B. **The Big Bang (for your buck) machine** – Uses old computer hardware with new software to repurpose otherwise obsolete hardware. Moderate specs, low in storage, low in processing, low in processing power. This machine does the same as above and a bit more processing power. This machine is a great value and does enough for low computer-intensive applications. One drawback, though, is higher power consumption.
C. **The Gamer's Delight** – Designed to run video games. High-end graphics, a moderate processor, medium speed RAM, and a large amount of SSD quick storage. This computer is all about frames per second and making sure that you get crystal clear graphics.
D. **The Virtual Boy** – Designed for running other operating systems inside of this PC. High Ram, Moderate quick storage,

a very quick processor, medium graphics. This computer is great for people who need to do many incredibly different things on one machine at any given time.

E. **The Workstation** – Designed for intensive content creation. High in ram, High in fast and slow storage, Great graphics, quick processor. This is where all of your creative juices flow, and the content that results from it will be handled with ease!

A and B work well for regular business use, C & D are for the enthusiast who wants performance but is not looking for a business application. The Workstation is what will help our 3D printing business. The workstation is built to meet the demands of the most demanding users. It has the fastest consumer processor available, a versatile motherboard with support for all the latest standards, gobs of RAM, and a cutting-edge solid-state drive. This will not only help you control the 3D printer it will also help do all the video editing you require to show the impact of parts that get 3D printed

By building the correct PC now, we can get working efficiently and effectively!

# What about a Laptop?

Many people may be asking why I focused specifically on tower PCs for this build. I do believe that a tower PC is better than a laptop for our purposes because that will force us to work in one place and keep everything together. Now if your idea requires that you are on the go to meet with people, I would encourage you to get a low powered laptop to keep the files and presentations on to show clients but not use that as the powerhouse creating all of the graphics, videos, and content that you need to make your business worthwhile. I believe that we can use laptops to be incredibly productive on the go, but we need to use them efficiently to do so. Making sure that you have a laptop that can handle simple tasks like word processing and internet browsing is enough for most needs. The used business market has plenty of corporate computers for incredibly cheap that make great auxiliary computers.

## Thinking About the Future

As we go through this process of designing our system, we need to take into account eh future. Think of the technological changes that could happen in the next few years and account for that. Make sure that as you are designing your new computer, you take into account the cost efficiency of the system and how the system will be in a few years. Will it still be able to do its designed purpose in 3 years? How about 5? You could always get a lower-end card and upgrade later or get a good motherboard and upgrade the processor later. Thinking about this now will allow you to make more financially responsible decisions now.

Additionally, another thing to think about is what is essential for the computer at this point? Will you need that water cooler right now? Do you need that new graphics card when you are doing web development? Once again, knowing exactly what your computer is going to be doing and what you can hold off on building out for a later date can help you control your costs now and give you something to look forward to in the future.

# My PC

This Section is designed in worksheet format to plan out the PC that works for you!

**MY PC TYPE** (From list above) _____

**Processor:** _____ Socket: _____

**Motherboard:** _____Type: _____
RAM Type: _____ CPU Socket: _____
IO Ports: _____
PCIE Layout: _____

**RAM:** _____
Type: _____ Amount: _____

**Storage:** _____
Type: _____ Amount: _____

**Secondary Storage:** _____
Type: _____ Amount: _____

**Case:** _____
Type: _____ PSU Included? _____

**Graphics card:** _____
Type: _____

**CPU cooler:** _____
Socket: _____

**Power supply:** _____
Type: _____ Wattage: _____
Rating: _____

**Peripherals:**

- _____
- _____
- _____
- _____
- _____

On the next page, I have included a chart to help you price out the machine.

| Item | Model | Store | Price |
|------|-------|-------|-------|
| Processor | | | |
| Motherboard | | | |
| RAM | | | |
| Storage | | | |
| 2nd Storage | | | |
| 3rd Storage | | | |
| 4th Storage | | | |
| Case | | | |
| Graphics Card | | | |
| Cooler | | | |
| Power Supply | | | |
| Peripheral | | | |
| Peripheral | | | |
| Peripheral | | | |
| Peripheral | | | |
| Peripheral | | | |
| Other | | | |
| Other | | | |
| | | TOTAL: | |

# Basic PC Assembly

In general, there are some basic steps that you should follow to assemble your new PC. I will detail some of those below.

When you have the new PC components items available, the next step is to Assemble the PC. PC Assembly is the most interesting part and also the most rewarding part when your system is up and running, all credits to yourself.

Vital Tools needed:

1. A screwdriver set

Other Optional Items:

2. Flashlight (So as to see the areas difficult to)
3. Antistatic wrist strap (this is to remove any static charges)

Firstly, discharge yourself of any static charges by touching the metal casing or attaching the other side of the antistatic wrist strap to the metal casing.

## Install the motherboard.

Ensure that the case is open and notice the motherboard standoffs that ought to have accompanied the case. They look like screw hole extenders. Insert the I/O Shield that came with your motherboard. That is the panel that mounts into the back of the case that merges with the ports on the rear of the motherboard. Find the holes on your motherboard that are for fastening the motherboard to the case and locate the comparing gaps on the motherboard fastening plate that correspond to the case. There should be holes in the case under every hole in your motherboard. If there is not, double-check to make sure that the case is the correct form factor. Place a standoff in every one of these openings on the plate and position the motherboard so as to allow you to see the holes in the highest point of the standoffs through the screw openings in the motherboard. Affix a screw through each of the motherboard screw openings into the standoffs underneath These screws ought to be cozy however not tight. With the motherboard in, we are now able to start installing different parts.

## Install the CPU.

Before you start, please read the manual provided with the motherboard/CPU carefully, understand the different parts, and the installation diagrams before proceeding. Remove the protective socket on the new socket protecting the pins on your motherboard

1.  Open the lever and lift the metal flap to install the CPU
2.  While carefully holding the CPU at the edges, look for the notch in the corner and match it up with the socket.
3.  Slowly lay down the CPU in the socket, before lowering the metal flap, and closing the socket lever to secure the CPU.

## Install the CPU heatsink.

We need to dissipate the high heat generated by the CPU so that it would not overheat and fry. I am recommending that you get ahold of some thermal paste that you can apply evenly on the CPU surface for better heat conductivity and dissipation. (To note: Intel boxed processors already come with their integrated thermal solutions, so it does not need extra) This thermal paste is essential if you want the heatsink to work properly and adequately dissipate all of the heat generated by the CPU.

1.  Align the heat sink onto the socket containing the CPU, with the fan cable orientated closest to the fan power connector on the motherboard that should be located close to the CPU socket and check for any entanglement.
2.  Press down on fastener caps with your thumb to install and lock them. Repeat this with the other three fasteners depending on the heatsink.
3.  Connect the fan cable from step 2 to the CPU_FAN connector located on the motherboard, which is located very close to the CPU. Tie up the excess cable to prevent interference with fan operation or other components.

## Install the Memory

With a new motherboard and fast processor, we will then need more RAM (random access memory) to enable and facilitate this faster performance. To insert the RAM modules, you have to loosen the clasps situated on every side of the memory slot. Align the RAM module in the socket, such as to match the indent located on the memory chip and the memory slot, for the right facing direction. Push down on the memory module until both clips refasten, and a click sound is heard. To change memory, press down both clips at the same time, and the RAM will come out easily.

TIP 1:  Put the RAM at the slot branded 'Bank 0'or 'DIMM 1'. If you do not, the system will think there is no memory available and won't boot up.

TIP 2: For newer systems supporting hyper-threading innovation, you are urged to utilize the double channel memory usefulness by setting two sticks of a similar memory on alternate spaces (i.e.: opening 1 and 3 or slot 2 and 4, frequently separated by shading also. Memory differentiation is proven to enhance performance as well as with these newer processes.

## Install the Power Supply

At the bottom or top of the case, there is a section where you can mount the power supply and secure the power supply using screws.

The power supply will consist of the following connectors:

- ATX power connector
- ATX_12V connector
- IDE or MOLEX power connectors
- SATA power connectors
- PCI-E Connectors
- FDD power connector

Look for the 20 or 24 pin ATX power connector and plug it into the motherboard allocated power slot. There may likewise be an extra four or eight pin power lead on the motherboard that should be connected, this connector, which is typically situated close to the processor, is just another quick addition to make. Plug the ATX_12V power connector there. Be sure to tie back all excess cables to make sure that there are no short circuits.

## Install the Hard-disks and DVD writers.

Hard disks and DVD ROM writers communicate with the CPU through data cables commonly SATA cables. If you have intention on using multiple hard disks, you must adjust the settings on the computer to inform the operating system, which is the main disk and the other supporting/additional disks. If not done properly, the system can get confused, and the computer may not boot at all.

1. First, remove the front casing of the computer, and remove the 5.25" plate to expose the front of the DVD drives that we will insert the unit into later.
2. Insert the disk writer into the hard disk bay we exposed earlier.
3. Hard disk drives and Solid-State drives go into a special hard disk bay that is usually located below the optical bays. You can find more information on how to properly mount the disk and where the bay is located from your case's instruction manual.
4. Insert the SATA cables into the hard disk or DVD writer data connector, noting the orientation of the notch on the side of the connector, to insert in the right direction. The remaining connector is to be connected to the motherboard.
5. Next, plug in the SATA power connector from the power supply each hard drive and optical drive. You will need to take note of the power connector orientation as well.
6. Finally, secure all disks and optical drive cables to make sure there are no short circuits.

## Install the Graphics Card

PCI Express video cards are more commonly used due to better data transfer performance and better resolution performance. PCI Express slots can be identified easily on the motherboard and are usually located adjacent to the CPU unit.

1. Prepare the card for insertion by removing all protective packaging, especially on the fans.
2. Remove one of the expansion card protector slots from the back of the case that lines up with the PCI Express slot that you wish to insert the card into.
3. Place the card into the opening with some power, and make sure that the card latches into place, with edges sticking out. Screw the newly inserted card at the highest point of the metal section.
4. If you discover that it has a power connector, then make sure to connect it immediately to a PCI Express power supply connector.

## Remaining Internal Connections

Now that we have connected the internals of the PC that are required to operate it, we still have to connect some of the internal components from the case to the motherboard. This step varies greatly between the different case models on the market, and your case's user manual will give you more insight into the way your case's wiring works.

a. Connect the audio cable from the DVD to the motherboard CD_IN connector (if required)
b. Connect the power/reset buttons, and signal indicators (those external blinking lights) to the F_Panel connector on the motherboard. (i.e., Power indicator, hardware indicator, or internal speaker). Your motherboard will also have the pinout

diagram in the user manual for this as well as the case. Make sure they line up!

c. Double-check on proper power connection to all hardware components
d. Install extra items such as front-mounted USB connectors, or sound ports.


## Final External Connections

Now that we have all of the internal connections on the PC finished, we can connect up the things that we use every day from our PC, like the screen, keyboard, and mouse.

e. Connect back the outer devices, including items like:
   i. Keyboard
   ii. Mouse
   iii. Monitor
   iv. Printer / Scanners
   v. Speakers
   vi. The external power supply cable


## Installing the Operating System

Finally, we arrive at the last stage of the PC assembly process. If you have done everything right, now is the time to sit back and savor the fruit of success. With the casing still open, and all external peripherals connected, turn on the computer and observe for any abnormality such as fans not spinning, or beeps alarms from the PC. If so, turn off the power and spend some time checking through the connections, and the manual for some tips on troubleshooting. Well, if you observed no abnormality till far, and you have seen the splash screen from the motherboard, you have succeeded in building your PC!

Next, you will want to get a USB disk or a DVD of the operating system you will want to install to the system. Plug it into the PC and turn it on. If all is well, you are greeted by the installation screen of your chosen operating system. If you are not, enter the BIOS of the system by pressing a key that is next to a 'Setup' or 'BIOS' label when the splash screen of the motherboard shows. From there, you can adjust the boot order of the devices attached to your PC. If you are using a USB or optical disk, make sure that the entry for that item is higher than the hard disk drive or solid-state drive you have installed in the system.

And just like that, you have built your money-making machine! Be sure to install all of the software you need on it and get it right to your liking, because you will be using it for a while!

By taking your time and building the computer that will last the next few years now, you can utilize the money that you have now and invest in a machine that will prove its worth not only in the business we are creating but also as technology changes as well. This can help us adjust to the newest technology as the time change.

# 7 GETTING THE WHEELS ROLLING
Developing a business model – what works best for you

We now have all the inputs on the Idea, product, or service we want to launch and the customer validation and feedback to start getting into the real stuff. Businesses require a substantial amount of groundwork to start. It is never a one-person show. We will use this chapter to do the following:

1) Developing a business model canvas
2) Develop a business plan
3) Develop the required legal documentation
4) Describe the different types of business as per the legal structures of the US
5) The requirement of the right team

## The Business Model Canvas

The detailed paperwork starts with creating a Business Model Canvas. Alexander Osterwalder proposed the Business Model Canvas based on his earlier book: Business Model Ontology. It outlines several prescriptions that form the building blocks for the activities. It enables both new and existing businesses to focus on operational as well as strategic management and marketing plans.

A well-developed business model canvas will help streamline the planning, development, and execution of your business. It should align everyone's objectives and eliminate inconsistencies between the various people who contribute to your business objectives.
The business model canvas defines the following:

## Key Partners

First, we have to identify the key partners need to conduct our business. Key Partners would include partners, suppliers, or collaborators on our business idea. It is helpful to target specific individuals and businesses, but it is also helpful to have general lines of businesses you want to focus on. Some of the key partners in our 3D printing business are the supplier of the 3D printing filament, the manufacturers we work with to create custom parts, and the clients.

## Key Activities

This is where we define the activities required to achieve the value proposition we have. We identify the key steps needed to be taken for our business to deliver on its promises and make sure development rolls out smoothly. To explain – for a product-driven business, a key activity may be learning about users and how to build a better product and manufacturing the product that you are producing. In our 3D printer business, our key activities are manufacturing custom parts as well as talking to the business owners and other customers on how we could improve. Another key activity is making connections in the Manufacturing industry and trying to apply 3D printing to new uses.

## Key Resources

To define the key resources, we must ask yourself what strategic assets do we need to launch and operate the business? For product-driven businesses, key resources include specialized talent in critical areas of expertise and intellectual property. For scope-driven businesses or businesses that create synergy around a Customer Segment, key resources must include knowledge about the target audience and a standard set of procedures for interaction and assistance with the group. Another thing that key resource covers are the machines and physical assets that we will need to acquire to make sure that we can run our business efficiently.

Additionally, one of the biggest key resources we can have here is our computer! It is our money-making machine that will allow us to actually carry out most of what needs to be done with our actual business processes. For our 3D printing business, we need to be able to procure modelling software, the 3D printers themselves, and the material needed for the 3D printer to operate.

## Unique Value Proposition

What is the business promising to its audience, and how does the defined product or service stand out? We must very carefully evaluate the uniqueness of our product or services and the reason why customers would prefer your product or service to alternative options. Once we have a list ready, we rank the propositions concerning the needs of our customers. Ordering this section will help us determine which value proposition is the highest priority and align our vision with the customers' needs.

The UVP statement should:
- Quickly and convey the value of your service or product
- Explain how your product or service is better than the

competition
- Talk about the benefits and features that define your product or service

It is not important to use superlative words, instead, include talking points that are carefully defined and factually correct

My UVP Statement is:

_____

_____

_____


There is a well-defined model detailed by Forbes, which can be used, it revolves around the 3Ds

- Discontinuous innovations – offer transformative benefits over the status quo by looking at a problem differently
- Defensible technology – offer intellectual property that can be protected to create an unfair competitive advantage
- Disruptive business models – yield value and cost rewards that help catalyze the growth of your business

## Customer Relationships

This starts with understanding how customers will interact with the business. Will they use the internet to connect, or will they get a personal contact, or will there be a call center approach where people are directed to a random salesperson? After establishing the type of relationship, it is important to write down guidelines for creating, maintaining, and growing the customer base. In our case of 3D printed parts and gifts, we need to form great relationships with business owners and shopkeepers that will be contracting us for custom parts. We will also need to work with people who want custom gifts. Additionally, we will need to educate the consumer on the new technology and the way that 3D printing technology can be applied to when you need a custom part produced.

## Distribution Channels

The section is all about how you reach the end customer. It is important to identify the most effective mediums to reach our audience. This should include the channels we use to communicate, sell, or provide service for customers. Make a list of the different channels that you plan on building a relationship with customers.

In most cases, since we are running an online business, this will be through a website or online shopping platform. Remember to think through the lens of the "customer journey." The channels with which you grab a customer's attention will be different from the way you onboard or support them. In order to find the best channel that will make the most money, you will need to think from the perspective of how a customer tries to find a business like yours. Do they go off the recommendation of friends? Do they search for it online? Do they go to the local business? In order to find the best distribution channel that works for you, you will need to think from the perspective of the customer. In our business, we will use the website to advertise the business as well as call local manufacturers to let them know about the new technology and schedule a demo.

## Customer Segments

It is essential to understand all facets of who the customer is. Do we have a single or multi-sided market? We must right detailed customer personas to define the target audience. Once this is done, we can move deeper to analyze who our individual customers are. With personas, one can investigate the problems and needs of our ideal customer and use these insights to refine the business model.

Use personas to gain insight into your customer segments by

- Collecting and displaying information about your customers' background, lifestyle, and behavioral practices

- Exploring the needs and desires of your customer and what they are using your product or service for
- Documenting the user journey

In our 3D business, we know that our ideal customer is a manufacturer who needs a custom part produced for their machine that broke. Based on that information, we know that people are looking for the quickest way to get the machine back online and the most effective way to make sure that the same issue does not happen again. By knowing this, we can do field testing to provide facts and statistics to show the benefits of 3D printed parts and their cost effectiveness. Likewise, you can use the information gathered to define further and document the way your customers think.

## Cost Structures

It is time to carefully consider how your Key Activities drive costs and analyze if these costs are aligned with your value propositions. It is also important to consider the type of costs that your business will be incurring. Are these costs fixed or variable? When scaling your business, will costs be linear or fixed? Will you have a subscription-based model where users pay a monthly rate for the services you provide or is it a onetime product they buy. It is good to ask your customers about this and gauge their interest in the different types of payment options. In our 3D business, it will be a single time contract for the design and manufacture of custom parts.

## Revenue Streams

Take a careful look at your different customer segments and value propositions and mentally map out the patterns that may occur. For example, Persona 1 may engage with Value Proposition 1, and 2 or Persona 2 may engage with Value Proposition 2 and 3. Carefully look at where your business is driving revenue and whether it aligns with your value propositions. How will you be making money? Will you license the technology out to other manufacturers? Are there any complementary goods and services you could offer to increase revenue? In this case, it would be helpful to look at and re-evaluate the services you offer to increase revenue with minimal effort. In our 3D printing business, we could also print custom small run part jobs using the same equipment and material, so it would make sense to offer this service as an extra source of income.

Again, this is a detailed activity and will require some time. Study as much as you can before you start writing the Business Model Canvas, this will be your core document to guide the business. The net has many resources to support your journey; some of our favorites are:

- https://canvanizer.com/new/business-model-canvas
- https://www.alexandercowan.com/business-model-canvas-templates/
- https://xtensio.com/how-to-create-a-business-model-canvas/

On the next page, you will have a business model canvas that you can fill out and use!

| Key Partners | Key Activities | Value Proposition | Customer Relationships | Customer Segments |
|---|---|---|---|---|
| | Key Resources | | Channels | |
| Cost Structure | | Revenue Streams | | |

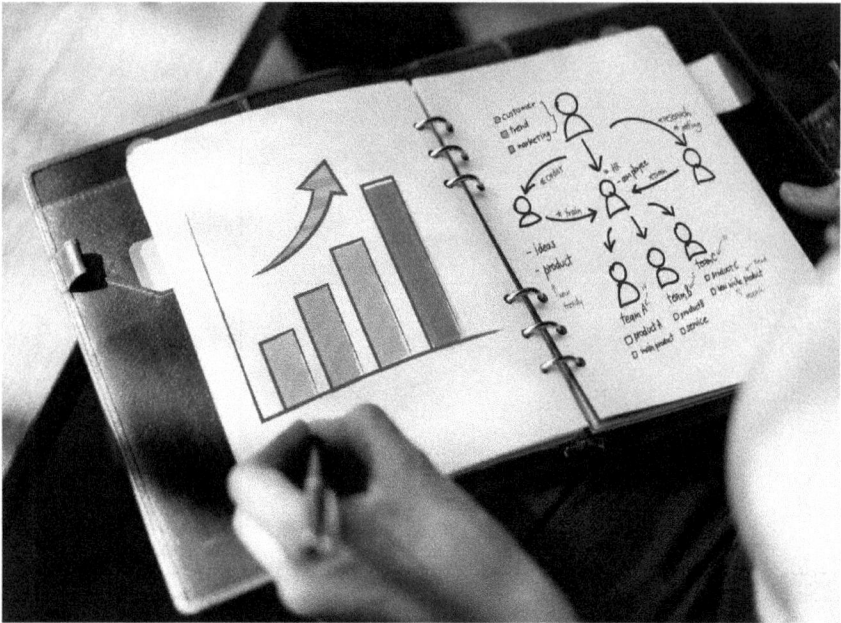

Figure 36: Making sure that your plans are written down holds you to them.

## The Business Plan

The next major step is to write the Business Plan.

Let us start with understanding the difference between a business model canvas and a business plan. The business model is the mechanism through which the company generates its profit, while the business plan is a document presenting the company's strategy and expected financial performance for the years to come. As evident, the business model is at the center of the business plan.

The business model describes how the company is positioned within its industry's value chain, and how it organizes its relations with its suppliers, clients, and partners to generate profits. The business plan translates this positioning in a series of strategic actions and quantifies its financial impact.

The business plan can be best defined as a communication tool, a snapshot of our business that is evolving all the time. It is primarily used for raising funds and is part of a broader communication strategy towards investors and other stakeholders.

The business plan must be written with the audience in mind. To highlight, are we looking for raising Angel funding or applying for a grant or applying for a loan or maybe raising Venture Capital. The plan will have to take the target audience in mind.

In general, business plans are written for people who will be loaning you money. These could be Angel Investors, bankers, or Venture Capitalists who are hoping to turn a profit in the long run. Take this into account when you write your plan, really accentuating the returns an investor could make by taking a chance on you or your idea.

It is very important to understand the audience we are making the business plan for. Fundraising will be a tough job. This audience is typically time-constrained, is constantly under pressure, as all of the people you meet with are all competing to find the next big winner. They are usually not experts on the technology but for sure are unforgiving. Do not be disappointed; this will happen given the amount of groundwork that has already been done for the project.

There are a few pointers to get this right the first time:
- Get the main message across in the first two paragraphs
- State clear potential rewards for the investor
- Explain business case in plain English
- Use your chance to make a great first impression

Guy Kawasaki defined the typical business plan and its structure in his book published in 2004, "The Art of the Start." It included the following parts:

1) Executive Summary
2) Problem – What is the problem?
3) Solution – What are you doing to solve it?
4) Business Model – How are you going to make money?
5) 'Underlying Magic' = technology – Competitive advantage
6) Marketing and sales – How are you reaching your customers?
7) Competition – Who is your competition?
8) Management team – Describe your team
9) Financial projections and key metrics – Balance Sheet, Profit and Loss, and cash flow
10) Current status, accomplishments to date, timeline and use of funds

One of the things that I like to tell people is only to do what you are good at! Farm everything else out to other people or hire them. You can focus on the creative focus of the business and delivering your product, and you can hire others to be able to do the more managerial and clerical work such as bookkeeping, accounting, and payroll.

Since the business plan is incredibly long, boring, and proliferated all over the internet, it is easier to go to many sites and have a live walkthrough of your plan as you complete it.

The following resources should help you do a great job at creating the business plan:

- Guy Kawasaki, "The Art of the Start", 2004
- Steve Blank & Bob Dorf, "The Start-up Owner's Manual", 2012
- Steven Gary Blank, "The Four Steps to the Epiphany", 2007
- Steve Blank's library of useful tools: www.steveblank.com

- LivePlan, www.liveplan.com
- Business model canvas download: www.businessmodelgeneration.com
- Alexander Osterwalder and Yves Pigneur: "Business Model Generation," 2010
- Paul Graham's Essays: http://paulgraham.com/index.html
- Y-Combinator Start-up Library: http://ycombinator.com/lib.html

*Figure 37: Legal documents can be scary, but they do not have to be!*

# Legal Documents

It is important to understand the legal framework that governs our business. We must now work towards developing our Legal Documents. Legal documents are very important as this is how we will be able to maintain our distinctive presence in the market. There is no shortcut here; legal non-compliance can be the single reason for the loss of total effort that has been put into the business. Negatives aside, the legal framework protects us and provides for intellectual property protection. This protection will include not only our products but also our brand and business, giving it a value that we can cash out with if so required.

It is prudent to engage a legal expert to ensure we get this done right. The legal part will have to be geography dependent. Defined by where the business is based and by where all you are doing business. The key documents that must be ready before we go to market include:

- Privacy Policy
- Terms of Service
- Shareholder Agreement
- Articles of Incorporation
- A contract for work, or Statement of Work
- Outside Contractor Agreement
- Non-Disclosure Agreement
- Intellectual Property Protection

## Privacy Policy

Your privacy policy is the document that you need to have anywhere in your website if you plan on collecting people's personal data or processing personally identifiable information. Due to recent legislation, it has become essential to detail exactly what information people are giving to you and how you are using it. The privacy policy is usually linked to on every page on your website from the footer.

## Terms of Service

The terms of service for your website is a contact that your website visitor agrees to when you sign up for the service. Terms of service generally detail all of the risks and limitations of the service you offer. This is the governing agreement of your services and allows you to set forward some terms that your clients agree to legally. This is, once again, something that can live on the footer of your website.

## Shareholder Agreement

It is essential that you document the creation of your company, especially when it comes down to who owns what. I know it is kind of morbid to think about if bad disagreements would arise as the company grows. A shareholder agreement does not need to be super complex; it just needs to be a legal document that everyone who holds a stake in your company can sign and agree to. In most single-person companies, you will not need an incredibly detailed document explaining who owns what since it is only one person doing the work, but it is still important to take care of.

## Articles of Incorporation

Your articles of Incorporation are the state-run legal documents that allow you to become a legal business in your respective state. I will detail these more in the different ways you can organize your company later in the chapter, but it is good to consult your local laws to see what you need to do to run a business legally.

## Statement of Work

Your Statement of Work is the contract used for some of the custom work that you may do for clients that are not like a lot of the other work you do. The statement of work contains some of the other terms and conditions specific to each client and can be customized to each need.

## Outside Contractor Agreement

There are some situations where you alone cannot handle all of the work presented to you. It may be required at times to hire people external to your organization to complete some specialized work. I would recommend that you think about this situation now and create the legal document to protect yourself, your company, your reputation and quality of work before the need arises and make sure you are ready for growth.

## Non-Disclosure Agreement

A non-disclosure agreement is an agreement that you have with other people that prohibits other people from telling the third party about your sensitive information that is essential to running your business in the same way you do. In some cases, a nondisclosure agreement allows you to communicate sensitive information to people with a serious penalty to them if they break the agreement.

## Intellectual Property Protection

Protecting your developments and inventions is essential for your continued success and brand identity. There are many forms of protection you can have for an idea, but I detail much more about this later in the book. It is, however, essential that you think about where you can use intellectual property protection now and file for papers if needed. In the rest of this section, I am going to attempt to detail some types of intellectual property and their various gotchas, but it may be lacking. I am not a lawyer, and there is no legal advice intended in this section, or book for this matter. I am merely regurgitating my bits of knowledge on this matter.

## Patents

A patent is a form of intellectual property which rewards people who invent a new and non-obvious:

- Process
- Method
- Machine
- Article of manufacture
- Composition of matter

In return for completely disclosing the invention, including how to practice the invention, a "legal monopoly" on the invention is granted to the people who invented the item for a specific time.

That legal monopoly is the right for the inventors to exclude other persons and businesses from making, using, offering for sale or selling, or importing the invention in the United States.

Once a patent application is prepared and filed and prior to issuance of a patent, the invention can be marked "patent pending" or "patent applied for".

While these have no legal significance and grant the inventors no legal rights, the designation tends to discourage other persons or businesses from copying the invention since a patent might issue on the invention granting the legal monopoly to the inventors.

There are two types of patents that are typically of interest to inventors, design patents and utility patents. A design patent protects the aesthetics or the appearance of the invention and is a much more limited legal monopoly than utility patents that protect the function of the invention. Therefore, utility patents are desirable over design patents where possible, though both design and utility patents can protect an invention.

In a utility patent, the most important area to check on the patent document is the claims section. In some cases, a patent document will detail all of the drawings of a specific invention, but the claims section may only protect the handle to which the device uses. In short, make sure you read the claims section of the patent document to make sure you know what is covered by the patent.

The time for which the legal monopoly is granted for a utility patent is 20 years from the filing date of a utility patent application; however, the legal rights do not begin until the patent issues. The period of time for which the legal monopoly is granted for a design patent is 14 years from the issue date.

Just since you got the patent, does not mean you are done paying the government. Utility patents require the payment of maintenance fees 3.5, 7.5, and 11.5 years following issuance to maintain the patent in force. Design patents require no maintenance fees to maintain the patent in force.

If, through the process of creating your business, you develop something you think is patentable, you should keep your invention a secret until you disclose the invention to a licensed patent attorney.

Additionally, if you are developing something novel, it would be smart to search the United States Patent and Trademark Office database to make sure the device does not exist.

Many foreign countries in which the inventor might decide to seek patent protection there is an "absolute novelty" requirement. This requirement means that if the invention is publicly disclosed (i.e., disclosed to people in a non-confidential manner) before the date in which you applied to that country, then the validity of any patent which would potentially issue on the invention in that country could be challenged later.

Many countries are members of the "International Treaty," also called the "Paris Convention." These countries allow inventors to claim "foreign priority" based on the filing date of the first-filed patent application in a member country, provided a patent application is filed in the member country within one year of the first filed patent application for utility patents, or within six months for design patent applications. The United States is a member of the International Convention and grants such priority based on a foreign patent application.

If you invent something, there are times when you need to file the patent to gain protection on it. The inventor must file a United States Patent Application within 1 year of:

- making an offer to sell the invention, even if the offer is not accepted and sometimes even when the invention is not yet manufactured or otherwise available.
- use of the invention in public (e.g., using the invention at work or in public on the street corner); or
- putting the invention in a printed publication that is circulated (e.g., a sales brochure, catalog, or a web site).

These are called "statutory bars," and if the year period expires without filing the United States Patent Application, the inventor is not permitted to file a patent application in the United States.

A provisional patent application can be filed in the United States which provides a disclosure, or description, of the invention, but does not have the formal requirements of a utility patent application.

If you develop a standard product, a patent application is a way to go to protect your intellectual property.

## Trademarks

The definition of a trademark is a pretty simple one. A trademark is just a sign of some kind that distinguishes a company from the rest of them. A trademark can come in many different forms. Maybe it is am image or a phrase. Anything that conspicuously distinguishes something from something else, in a sense, can technically be a trademark.

What about those little circles with the "TM" and "R" in them? What do they mean? The "TM" refers to a trademark, and the "R" refers to a registered trademark. While they serve as gentle reminders that the trademark is protected by law, they are not necessary. There are both unregistered and registered trademarks out there, the latter carrying more weight in a court of law. Most of the trademarks you see on TV and in magazines are registered.

Just as with physical property, intellectual property – when handled in court – is dealt with based on its jurisdiction. As with patents, these trademarks are handled at the United States Patent and Trademark Office, or USPTO for short.

One of the interesting things about trademarks, though, is that you can register trademarks that only have jurisdiction in your state at your Secretary of State's office. This will legally protect your brand in your specific state, but not the country as a whole.

There are five basic kinds of trademarks: distinctive, arbitrary, suggestive, descriptive, and generic. On the other hand, some symbols can never be used in trademarks, like national flags. It is also important to note that national and international trademark laws vary, so especially if you are conducting business overseas, you should be aware of that.

A trademark can open your company up to all kinds of business and separate it from the pack, but if it is not formed carefully, it may misrepresent and misdirect your company. So, choose your trademark intelligently and make sure you understand the law backing it up so that you can put it to good work.

A trademark can help you protect your brand, logo, product names, or any other esoteric visual differentiator that consumers can connect to your brand.

## Copyrights

Copyrights are another form of intellectual property protection whereby someone who creates an original work can protect it under the law with their authorship as 'owning' the document. A copyright can be assigned to an artwork, book, or work that is the creative physical product that someone is offering. Interestingly enough, software falls under this type of intellectual property, since copyrights protect works that are fixed in a "tangible medium of expression" ergo, a computer. Software falls under this category because of the creativity in how the code for the program is written since there are many ways to accomplish something in code. Copyrights do not need to be registered but allow you to transfer legal fees to the other party if you sue and win.

The difference between a copyright and a trademark is the fact that the trademark is basically for brand images, while the copyright is for the branding and different aspects that tell your brand apart. Copyrights are valid for your lifetime plus 70 years.

## Trade Secrets

A trade secret is something that allows your business to do business the way it can and does not fall into any of the other categories. Think of secret recipes of things. If you would put that in a patent, everyone would know the exact formula to make the product and would do that after the patent expired rendering your advantage useless. With a trade secret, the term of protection is indefinite, as long as the secret remains a secret. Interestingly, trade secrets are not registered at any central agency; rather, they are self-enforced under legally binding non-disclosure agreements.

## Getting a Patent

Do it yourself patents can be a great alternative for those who cannot afford to dish out thousands of dollars for a patent lawyer. Filing your patents can be done, but there are some challenges. While not impossible, the biggest drawback of doing it yourself is that you do not have the luxury of professional advice.

The advantages of filing your patents are hard to overlook. As previously mentioned, it certainly can save you money. Also, by doing it yourself, you can learn several valuable skills, particularly research. The central step in preparing to file a patent is to verify that the invention is actually patentable, meaning it both qualifies to be patented and has not been previously patented. You will also need to give an explanation of all areas of your invention so as to file your patent. Some steps in the process are easy; others might be extremely difficult. As with all new endeavors, you will most likely succeed by trial and error. However, by taking it one step at a time and studying the process as much as possible, you can reduce or possibly even eliminate the errors before they occur.

The following are fundamental steps on filing your patent:

1. Retain careful documentation of your invention. It is important to type up or write down the record of the innovation procedure in a note pad or a similar format. Sign and date every passage and have two solid observers sign also.

2. Ensure Your Invention is eligible or meets the criteria for Patent Protection. However, you will need to show that your invention is new (not previously patented), non-obvious, and useful.

3. Determine the commercializablity of your new technology. Before you spend the time and money to file a patent application, you need to examine the market you would like to enter to make sure it will be profitable to file the patent in the long run.

4. To be certain of how innovative your invention is, conduct a very critical in-depth Patent Search. To ensure your development is new, you need to search for all the prior art in your field. This includes looking into U.S. and international patents, as well as different periodicals like academic and industry-specific journals in order to discover related developments.

5. Talk to an intellectual property attorney, they will be able to help you get all of the legalese and paperwork processed to get your application ready to go.

6. Get ready and File an Application with the United States Patent and Trademark Office. This step allows you to always have a decision when filing with the USPTO: you can file a full-scale normal patent application (RPA), or you can file a provisional patent application (PPA) on the invention. Filing a provisional patent application permits you to guarantee patent pending status for the innovation but it includes only part of the full protections of a patent, and you still have to file the full patent within one year. Your patent application will consist of a detailed account of the invention, telling or illustrating the procedures on how to create it, and an informal drawing.

## Patent Searches

Any inventor should conduct a free patent search to determine the patentability or manufacturability of his or her invention. Doing this search before you invest significant time and effort into the research and development of a product. Making sure something like what you hope to develop does not exist will save you a headache down the road when you try to patent something or get caught in legal trouble. Patent searches have traditionally been limited to a search of the Patent Office's records of prior patents and publications. The recognition of business method patents combined with the assistance of the Internet made it both necessary and possible for patent searches to evolve and become easier to do, especially online. Still, patent searches begin in the electronic databases of the various Patent Offices worldwide.

Inventors need not immediately solicit the help of a professional to conduct a prior patent search, although they will do it much more thoroughly. Inventors can get a general idea of the landscape and can do the work themselves by searching for patent search Web sites online. For an inventor to be able to start his or her patent search, they need first to access the U.S. Patent and Trademark Office Database.

Additionally, Patent and Trademark Depository Library (PTDL) is a library designated by the (PTO) to receive and house copies of US patents and patent and trademark materials, to make them available to the public, and to disseminate both patent and trademark information. A library must meet specific requirements and promise to fulfill certain obligations to be designated as a PTDL. At these PTDLs, patents and word mark trademarks may be searched. Patent and Trademark Depository Librarians cannot give any legal advice, nor can they perform the free patent search for someone.

For many inventors, it is important to avoid spending thousands of dollars in a patent application only to have it refused. In some instances, only certain elements of the proposed invention, but not all, will be patentable. Conducting a prior patent search allows the inventor to identify the patentable elements and file a patent application, which avoids the problem embodiments.

Seven steps to conducting a free patent search at Patent and Trademark Depository Library (PTDL):

## Index to the U.S. Patent Classification

Begin with this alphabetical subject index to the Manual of Classification. Look for common terms describing the invention and its function, effect, end-product, structure, and use. Note class and subclass numbers.

## Manual of Classification

Locate class and subclass numbers in the Manual. Note where the terms fall within the US Patent Classification System. Scan the entire class schedule, paying attention to the dot indent. Revise the search strategy as needed.

## Classification Definitions

Read the definitions to establish the scope of class(es) and subclass(es) relevant to the search. The definitions include important search notes and suggestions for further searching.

## Browse Patent Titles and Abstracts

Check if you are on the right path; retrieve and browse through titles of patents and published applications in the given class and subclass. Or redirect the search: retrieve lists of patents and published applications containing applicable keywords; note their class and subclass numbers and go back to Step 2. Remember that Patents BIB includes bibliographic information for patents from 1969 to present and published patent applications from 2001 to the present. WEST includes the full text of patents from 1971 to the present. USPTO databases on the Web include the full text of patents from 1976 and images (searchable only by class or number) from 1790 to the current week, plus published applications from 2001 to present.

## Retrieve Subclass Listing

Once you have identified the relevant classes and subclasses, obtain a list of all patent numbers granted from 1790 to the present and all published applications from 2001 to the present for every class and subclass to be searched.

## Official Gazette – Patent Section

Go to the Gazette and look for exemplary claim(s) and a representative drawing for all patents on the list(s) to eliminate patents unrelated to the invention. For published applications, view the complete document on-line.

## Complete Patent Document

Search the complete text and drawing(s) of closely related patents to determine how different they are from the invention you have created.

Having a good legal partner is almost a "must-have" for any business. We would emphasize on ensuring this is well covered. Some resources that we like on the net include:

- https://www.entrepreneur.com/article/236967
- http://smallbusiness.chron.com/legal-paperwork-needed-start-business-2305.html

*Figure 38: There are many different legal structures, and they each have different perks, just like the different pieces in chess*

# Legal Structure

Business can be organized in many legal structures; each structure has its advantages and is well suited to a certain type of work. It is important to get the right Legal Structure for the business we plan.

The legal team that advised on the set of documents would be well placed to help in getting the business registered with the right type. The various types used in the US include:

## Sole Proprietorship

A Sole Proprietorship is one individual or married couple in business alone. Sole proprietorships are the most common form of business structure. This type of business is simple to form and operate and may enjoy greater flexibility of management, fewer legal controls, and fewer taxes. However, the business owner is personally liable for all debts incurred by the business, which means that you could be sued for all you are worth if something happens. There is no legal separation from business and personal assets.

## General Partnership

A General Partnership is composed of 2 or more persons (usually not a married couple) who agree to contribute money, labor, or skill to a business. Each partner shares the profits, losses, and management of the business, and each partner is personally and equally liable for debts of the partnership. Formal terms of the partnership are usually contained in a written partnership agreement.

## Limited Partnership

A Limited Partnership is composed of one or more general partners and one or more limited partners. The general partners manage the business and share fully in its profits and losses. Limited partners share in the profits of the business, but their losses are limited to the extent of their investment. Limited partners are usually not involved in the day-to-day operations of the business. Filing with the Secretary of State is required.

## Limited Liability Partnership (LLP)

A Limited Liability Partnership (LLP) is similar to a General

Partnership except that normally a partner doesn't have personal liability for the negligence of another partner. This business structure is used mostly by professionals, such as accountants and lawyers. Filing with the Secretary of State is required.

## Limited Liability Limited Partnership (LLLP)

A Limited Liability Limited Partnership is a Limited Partnership that chooses to become an LLLP by including a statement to that effect in its certificate of the limited partnership. This type of business structure may shield general partners from liability for obligations of the LLLP. Filing with the Secretary of State is required.

## Corporation

A Corporation is a more complex business structure. A corporation has certain rights, privileges, and liabilities beyond those of an individual. Doing business as a corporation may yield tax or financial benefits, but these can be offset by other considerations, such as increased licensing fees or decreased personal control. Corporations may be formed for-profit or nonprofit purposes. Filing with the Washington Secretary of State is required.

## Nonprofit Corporation

A Nonprofit Corporation is a legal entity and is typically run to further an idea or goal rather than in the interests of profit. Many nonprofits serve the public interest, but some engage in private sector activities. If your nonprofit organization is or plans to raise funds from the public, it may also be required to register with the Charities Program of the Washington Secretary of State. Charitable activities may require additional registration. Contact the Secretary of State for more information.

## Limited Liability Company (LLC)

One or more individuals or entities form a Limited Liability

Company (LLC) through a special written agreement. The agreement details the organization of the LLC, including provisions for management, assignability of interests, and distribution of profits and losses. LLCs are permitted to engage in any lawful, for-profit business or activity other than banking or insurance. Filing with the Secretary of State is required.

## Massachusetts Trust

A Massachusetts Trust is an incorporated business with the property being held and managed by the trustees for the shareholders. The trustees are considered employees since they work for the trust. Filing with the Secretary of State is required.

## Trust

A Trust is a legal relationship in which one person, called the trustee, holds the property for the benefit of another person, called the beneficiary.

## Joint Venture

A Joint Venture is formed for a limited length of time to carry out a business transaction or operation.

My Business will be legally structured as a

_____.

I will need the following documents to get started:

1. _____
2. _____
3. _____
4. _____
5. _____
6. _____
7. _____
8. _____
9. _____
10. _____

I need to register with:

_____

_____

_____

## Additional Information

Understanding the structures and then using the available legal options to register the business is an integral part of launching. There are resources available on the net which will help us understand this better. But a good legal team cannot be substituted for reading online. We can get basics from:

- http://bls.dor.wa.gov/ownershipstructures.aspx
- https://www.usa-corporate.com/start-us-company-non-resident/entity-types/
- https://www.shopify.com/guides/united-states-of-america/business-structures

Once we have done all the legal work, it is evident to us that a business needs a team. The importance of having the right people with you cannot be overemphasized. Be it suppliers, advisors, partners for sales or marketing, or just people to make sure you are not going insane; everyone must be carefully aligned with our business objectives. It is often said that the best partners are the ones who are at the same stage of business as you are. For example, if you want an advertising agency, do not go to the largest; look for a creative mind who is starting up a new venture. The chances of him creating something out of the blue and remarkable with you are high. Not that large agencies are bad or anything, just that they may be very conservative for a startup like ours.

# 8 MAKING YOUR IDEA A REALITY

The supply chain and the experts – the cogs in your wheel

To be successful in business, you will require an efficient supply chain. You will have to look for the right manufacturer, distributor, or supplier of goods you require to service your customers. It is important to get the right manufacturer or supplier for your product idea. Even if you plan to manufacture yourself, you will require raw material to manufacture with. In some cases, though, such as making software, you will not specifically need a material to manufacture with, but you will need infrastructure to support the software running in the cloud.

The other things that you will require will include people to help you do the daily stuff. Someone to make and maintain your website and your social media or marketing efforts. If you plan for customer engagement through a blog, then you may require a specialized content person, potentially through a freelancer or a firm. All this needs to be carefully planned to ensure that the right partnerships are created, and the best value can be derived from these partnerships. In most cases, you can do this yourself, but it may be worthwhile to investigate having other people take up some of the slack rather than overstretching yourself.

Figure 39: *Look for the one that stands out!*

## Finding the Right People

The starting point will once again be talking to the right set of people. Touch base with as many senior executives and entrepreneurs that you can find. People with supply chain experience, manufacturing experience, or with strategy background should be a good bet for understanding the complex supplier ecosystem. Your legal team will also come in handy as each supplier/partner will have to be integrated into a proper contract.

Let us start with finding a supplier – many entrepreneurs find themselves hitting a brick wall and losing momentum when it's time to source products. Whether it be manufacturing your own product or finding suppliers to purchase wholesale products from, good manufacturing partners are not always easy to find. One must find answers to many questions before a supplier is finalized. Let us find some of these questions and answers them for you.

## The Basics – Determining What We Need

Within the term suppliers, we are referring to anyone that can provide you with products and inventory. This encompasses manufacturers, wholesalers, and distributors.

You will find a lot of useful resources online just by searching Google. However, before you start your big search, there are a few things you should consider.

First, you should determine what type of supplier or manufacturing partner you are looking for. Determining the supplier type will help in defining the terms/keywords you need to use in your research. There is a lot of literature defining what best fits your business model. Should you Make, Subcontract, Wholesale or Dropship your products? The industry today has successful examples of all types of sourcing.

There are a few different scenarios for this search:

- You may need a manufacturer to produce your own product idea
- You may need a supplier, who may also be a manufacturer, wholesaler, or distributor to purchase already existing brands and products
- You may be looking for a drop shipper to deliver items and fulfill orders of previously existing brands and items

The second big question is Domestic vs. Overseas Suppliers.

## Domestic vs Overseas

One of the questions people ask when looking for suppliers is whether you want to keep everything in your home country or send it overseas. Abroad can allude to any area, not in the continent you live on, but usually, in today's context with lots of contract manufacturing shifting to Asia, this leads to suggesting Asian states such as Taiwan, India, and China.

Most industry people will tell you that it is much less expensive to source your items from overseas. But this decision should be taken with many factors in mind. It should not be just a matter of startup costs and cost per unit.

Together, domestic and abroad sourcing have their pros and cons of which will be detailed below.

*Figure 40: Domestic sourcing often sends semi-trucks full of your stuff across the country!*

## Domestic Sourcing

This type of sourcing is from within your home country. Contracting is often done with a vendor close to home.

**Advantages**

- Higher quality and standards
- Simpler correspondence with no language obstruction
- Showcasing intrigue of being made in North America
- It is easier to confirm trustworthy producers
- Quicker transportation time
- Governmentally recognized intellectual property protections.
- More regulations and safeguards against payment default.
- Boosting the US manufacturing economy

**Disadvantages**

- The cost of production is high
- There is less of a choice of available products. (Many things simply aren't made in North America any longer)

*Figure 41: Shipping crates coming from all ends of the world!*

## Overseas Sourcing

Overseas or abroad sourcing is usually more popular and involves making sure that the shipment gets across the world to your doorstep.

### Advantages

- The cost of production is low and cheap.
- Large number of manufacturers in all industries willing to work with you
- One-stop industries like Alibaba have made it simple to explore manufacturers and wholesalers

### Disadvantages

- Lower quality noticed by consumers.
- Lower standards in labor and manufacturing safety
- Intellectual property theft could occur where bad manufacturers manufacture your product in the 'off hours' of factory time under the table.Language, cultural, or time differences could make it harder to communicate properly.
- It is difficult and expensive to check manufacturers or distributers and visit on-site
- Shipping time is very long
- Social and cultural diversities in strategic business policies.
- Item importation and customs authorization

Therefore, it is quite clear that the decision to source locally or from overseas is also not just a cost decision but is quite a complex multifactor decision as well. It comes down to each use case as to which is right for you.

I will source whatever I need for the business (Circle one)

Domestically                    Overseas

# Where to Begin Your Search

Once you have decided on local or overseas sourcing, it is now time to start looking for the right supplier. Where would you find a list? Naturally, the internet is a great place to start looking for your supplier, however, there are still many other places that can aid with the search

## Directories

These directories comprise of details for hundreds or if you like, thousands of producers, wholesalers, and providers Beneath, I have rattled off a couple of the most well-known ones for both local and abroad suppliers:

Domestic Online Directories

- ThomasNet
- Makers Row
- MFG

Overseas Online Directories

- Oberlo
- Alibaba
- AliExpress
- IndiaMart
- Bambify
- Sourcify

# Google

Searching for suppliers this way is the tricky one in the last bunch of years, as we've gotten acquainted with having the option to effectively look through Google and find what we're searching for in the initial few results that pop up. Nonetheless, numerous providers have not stayed up with the web and Google's algorithm is usually not consistent. Their websites are generally old, provide inadequate data, lack up to date product information. And are likely not SEO optimized. Therefore, these websites will inherently not show up in Google search even though they may be the thing you are looking for! These suppliers focus more on the production and shipment as opposed to online marketing. Many of them operate on word of mouth publicity and against keeping their sites google compliant.

So how would you discover providers on Google? For this to happen effectively, you will have to investigate page ten of Google search lists, and past. You will additionally need to utilize an assortment of search terms. For instance, words like discount, distributor, and merchant might be utilized reciprocally, so you should scan for every one of them.

It might assist you with making yourself acquainted with Google's tools to improve the nature of your searches, and consequently the outcomes.

# Local Library

You may also want to consider dusting off your library card and heading to your local library. Many libraries pay monthly subscription fees for online business and manufacturer directories that you normally would not have access to, or you would have to pay a large amount of money for, like the Scotts Online Business Directory. These directories contain profiles for many manufacturers, wholesalers, and distributors in North America, depending on the exact directory.

It is compulsory give your local library a call ahead of time or check on their website to determine if they have access to these types of private directories and whether commercial usage is allowed. A lot of other libraries also have the information about many databases they have access to on their website as well.

## Referrals

People like sharing things that worked well for them. This is the case as well with suppliers. Having people refer you to what they found worthwhile can help you form great connections. Additionally, some suppliers may be inclined to give you better rates based on who referred you!

As you work through working with various suppliers, if as much as they are not the correct fit, ensure that they point you in the right direction of some other suppliers or vendors that may be able to assist you. Since they are in the business, they will be able to help allude you to somebody else that may work better for your business.

## Additional Research Tips

Another conceivable method to look for item providers is via scanning for your items by their NAICS code.

NAICS stands for the North American Industry Classification System, and basically each and every industry and item you can consider is joined to a NAICS code. At times makers and providers may list their items by the NAICS code which can make your product manufacturers and suppliers easier to find, especially if you are using professional directories.

The NAICS directory can be found at your local library or on the Internet at:

– https://www.census.gov/eos/www/naics/

I Will Research Suppliers using these sources:

1. _____
2. _____
3. _____

# Requesting A Quote

Once you have found a suitable supplier, how do you approach them?

The question we need an answer to, of course is just "How Much" will it cost. But before we ask the direct questions, many times referred to as an RFQ, or request for quote, there are several things we need to be covered. Take a few minutes to plan out what you want to say and the questions you need to ask or your supplier surrounding their own company, capabilities, or previous experience. Planning your email will increase your chances that you will receive a response and the correct information.

Here are a few important questions to consider for your email:

What is your minimum order quantity? - Also referred to as an MOQ, you want to make sure their minimums are manageable for you and that you can afford them. This minimum order quantity can vary wildly depending on the product and the supplier, so it is important to ask upfront.

What is your sample pricing? - You'll likely want samples to inspect before making a full order. This way, you know that you are getting a quality product before putting your money on the line in a full order.

Sample pricing ranges, depending on the product and supplier. Some suppliers that receive many requests may charge the full retail pricing, others will offer you samples at a discounted rate, and some may even send you samples for free.

What is your production pricing? - One of the most important questions is how much your products will cost. You would probably like to ask for pricing for several quantities to get a sense of it and how they do discounted pricing at higher quantity levels. In addition, you will want to make sure that there is not a per-unit production cost or surcharge added onto the unit cost.

What is your turnaround time? - Knowing how long it will take to produce your order is an important consideration and depending on your exact business, time can be critical. This will also define your minimum stock levels. That is, if it takes minimum 30 days to make then we must always keep 60-day inventory. You do not want to be caught off-guard with being out of stock on a product that customers want.

What are your payment terms? - Many suppliers will require new businesses to pay for the full order upfront. This is important to know since inventory is a major cost for e-commerce startups. You may want to also ask if they provide payment terms for future orders as well.

Suppliers get bombarded with email quote requests all the time from flaky buyers that are just 'kicking the tires' so it's not unusual for many suppliers not to reply to every request. A lack of supplier responsiveness is a common complaint from new e-commerce entrepreneurs.

So how do you avoid being ignored? There are a few things that you should avoid when you reach out to suppliers for the first time:

Long emails - Your first email to a manufacturer should be clear and concise. Avoid telling too much about your story and background. The first email should be purely to assess potential fit at a high level. Focus on what suppliers care about the most like the details of what you are trying to source.

Asking for too much - Requests are not always easy for the supplier to produce. It is important to ask for a few prices for multiple quantities but avoid asking for too much or too many quotes. Stick to asking for what you absolutely need to assess the fit between you and the supplier.

Asking for too little - If you ask for a quote well below the supplier's minimum order you risk being met with silence. If you are unsure if your request is too small, consider giving them a quick call or send a quick one question email prior to asking what their minimum order is.

Finally, if you are contacting a supplier from overseas, keep in mind that in many cases, they may be using translating programs to translate your email as well as their reply. Keeping your emails short, concise, well formatted, and spelling error free will not only help the manufacturer, but it will ultimately provide you with better replies and answers. Also, when asking your questions, it is best to number your questions, so that they can easily reply to each number, keeping the questions and communication clean and organized.

Here is an example of an email I might send out:

Hi,

My name is ABC and I am from XYZ company.

I am interested in placing an order for Widget A. I just have a few questions beforehand:

1. What is your minimum order quantity?
2. What is your cost per unit at the minimum order as well as if I were to order 3x your minimum order?
3. What are your payment terms for new customers?

I would also like to order a sample of Widget A to verify quality. Can you please send me the cost of the sample, including shipping to:

ABC
80 Startup Way, Suite 4
Anywhere, IL, USA
00000

Thank you,
ABC

As you can see from the sample above, it is short, concise and its goal is to make sure at a high level that there is a fit between us. I have also set myself up to immediately order a sample unit, should there be a good fit between us. Once I have received the samples and I am happy with them, I can then start getting into more detail knowing I'm not wasting their time or mine.

## Negotiating Minimums

If you are looking for a supplier for the first time, you're going to quickly learn about 'Minimum Order Quantities' (MOQ's). It is not uncommon for a manufacturer to require a commitment to purchase hundreds or even thousands of units for your first order depending on the product and manufacturer.

MOQ's make it difficult when you have limited funds, or simply want to play it safe by starting small to test the market before making larger purchases. The good thing is that MOQ's are almost always negotiable.

Before you begin negotiating, the first step is to understand why the supplier has imposed a minimum. Is it because there is a lot of work upfront? Do they prefer to work with larger buyers? Are raw material costs significantly cheaper in bulk? Understanding the reasons behind the minimum will help you better understand their position and allow you to negotiate and propose the best counteroffer.

After you have a better understanding of your supplier's position, you can offer a lower order quantity. Compromises can include giving the supplier a deposit for a larger order, but just producing small amounts at a time or paying a higher price per unit.

## Have You Found Your Supply Partner?

Sourcing suppliers and manufacturers is a unique process, and for many, a new experience. Trying to locate suppliers that are a good fit is a critical decision for your new business and are not always easy to find. It is easy to get frustrated when you hit dead ends or brick walls but, in most cases, it just requires a little more patience and perseverance to find the perfect partner for your new business.

Once you have the supplier in place it is time to look for partners that will help you with other important things that you are not as good at. One of the key aspects of creating your online venture will be building a website. Getting a reliable partner who would not only understand your business need but will also come up with a feasible model that does not cost a fortune is important here.

*Figure 42: All the Code!*

# Creating your product

In many software or technology startups, it is often the case where a developer or coder will start from scratch to create a product that the company will soon offer. Understanding the tools and technologies available to you will make life easier.

## What do you need to code?

In a lot of cases, people believe that you need to code every single thing that your product will offer, when in fact there will be vendors that can provide a specific part or integration of your project at a much lower cost and greater features than you would be able to launch. There are many popular invoicing solutions for clients out there, and they could do a great job at their specific job at a fraction of the price.

Another great advantage of this type of relationship with a vendor is the fact that this code is something that you will not have to maintain and fix issues with. You can tell them your issue and they will usually fix it as part of the contract they have with you. This takes liability off of you as a seller making sure that you are spending your time doing other lucrative things.

Of course, everything isn't perfect, and some issues may arise with working with another vendor for software, such as incompatibilities as both products develop separately, vendor support or lack thereof, and some intellectual property claims on code that you cannot add to your repertoire of property.

## Coding Languages

Knowing the result of your product and where its use cases will be originating from will truly help you determine how to properly develop your product and what languages to use.

Depending on how users will consume your product, whether that is web, application, in person, or via phone, you will need to research the specific platforms to accurately determine the coding languages needed to properly develop a futureproof and robust solution that you will be able to grow and scale with. I could ramble for hours on this, but I feel like I would do a disservice to anyone reading this book years from publication for the technology may have changed and it would no longer be on the cutting edge.

Making sure that your platform development research is solid here will allow you to be able to develop a great solution.

## Know your tools

Like any master of a craft, you need to know what tools are out there for doing your job well. There are a plethora of different coding tools, environments, and doodads that all seem to offer some sort of benefit over the competition. Nonetheless, for the sake of no biasness, I will detail categories of tools that will help you create your product.

If you will be creating APIs, or Application Passing Interfaces, having a testing application is indispensable. APIs are the backend programs responsible for serving the same data to all forms of devices such as mobile phones, tablets, and web applications. There are many free applications available to be able to do this such as Postman.

If you are creating databases, a database administration software is essential to making sure that your database queries and table structures will work correctly in the final product. There are many tools available to do this in a number of architectures, so make sure you adequately research a tool that reflects the needs of your business.

If you will be creating multimedia content, having a good photo editor and video editor is great to creating quality content, but is not as essential as a lot of the other tools mentioned before. Most paid content creation programs streamline the process of content and multimedia creation, but do not necessarily make you more creative. It is as much how much you want to put into learning a platform as you want to get out.

On a final note of this section, make sure all your tools are compatible with the language and architecture of your choosing. Incompatibilities will only create frustrations down the road.

## Development Environments

Now the keen among you may have noticed that I have left out a key part of the tools needed to create your product: the development environment! This is the entire platform that you will utilize to create the code for the program you make as well as test and run it. There will obviously be more documentation on the specific environments for different platforms, but they all follow a relatively common stack of tools that I have detailed below.

- Editor: This is the program that actually allows you to view and edit the files of the program. Most editors on the market have syntax highlighting, which can point out different parts of the code for you to help spot syntax errors by sight and make your life a little less boring because now you can look at pretty colorful code.
- Linter: This is like spell check for code and will alert you to syntax errors. This is often bundled in with a good editor.
- Debugger: This is the tool that allows you to take a true look at the inner workings of your code and find the errors that lie under the hood when testing your program.
- Compiler: The compiler is the program that creates the executable files that the end user runs from the source code that you wrote. You would not want everyone having a key to your house, right? The computer is the locksmith that prevents people from seeing the innerworkings of your program.
- Server: In some cases, a server may be necessary to see the files generated from the compiler. This could be on your local machine and have the ability to work anywhere. Once again, this depends heavily on your chosen platform.
- Additional tools: On some specific platforms there may be additional tools that are needed to run tests such as a device simulator or an event handler. Research your chosen platform for specific instructions.

As you can see, the development environment is essential to making sure that a developer can work efficiently and effectively. Make sure you do adequate research on this and take all potential tools you will need for the project into account early on, so you do not need to waste time learning how to use new tools midway through the project.

## Code Tracking

As you develop your product, you will start creating versions of code—and a lot of it! Code tracking and revision history is very important to make sure that you keep yourself, your project, and your code organized. There are many popular code management tools out there that will let you know exactly what changes you have made in a version, and these will be indispensable as you grow to a bigger company.

One catch to watch out for is making sure that some code management services do not make your proprietary code public for anyone to download. This could be a security risk and an issue when it comes to getting intellectual property protection.

## Project Management

As with any project, managing the project well will allow for the project to succeed. Any project can only be successful if the people behind the project implement proper project management skills.

Project management may sound like a complicated term, and it really is, as it involves the process of organizing the different factors involved in creating and completing a project.

All projects should start out with a good plan so that the project creator would know the things required for the project to proceed as well as the necessary timeframe within which these requirements must be accomplished. Hopefully, most of this information can be gleaned from the immense amount of market research and business planning you have done. The project plan should identify the scope of the project and the people accountable for the various aspects of the project.

One of the things you may be wondering is how this section is different from the other business creation plans we have developed.

This section details more along the lines of the projects needed to develop the things you sell—moreso on the research and development side of things. In order to develop the actual product, careful planning is needed to ensure you work efficiently.

The plan should include the costs involved in managing the project including the costs involved in hiring human resources and materials for the project to be completed. A good and realistic plan will enable the project manager to fulfill the project requirements on time and in an efficient manner.

Like every other project, a project management plan should include a good plan for human resources as they will be the best resources the project manager can have. Another important aspect is the communications plan not only between and among the project manager and the employees or workers. It should also include a good communication system with the outside world.

The project manager should be more wary of a good communication plan especially if the project has a very great impact with a certain group of people or stakeholders. If this is the case, the project manager should also make sure to include a public relations plan as well as a communications plan in cases of emergency or negative reaction from the public.

Risk management should be one of the most important aspects of the project plan. The project manager should avoid being reactionary whenever emergencies or negative publicity comes up. To avoid this and to become proactive he should establish a contingency plan for possible situations and develop responses to risk in any form. Carefully taking time to plan here could allow for quicker recovery once an unexpected risk becomes a reality.

One of the most challenging projects to handle or to manage is a software project because of the technical emergencies that may happen, the sudden changes in costs and the sudden changes in technical people involved in the software project.

However, a project manager should always be prepared for any issue for any type of project they are handling. The best thing to do is to prepare a very efficient project management plan so that they are not caught unaware of very important aspects of the project.

## Getting Online

One of the big things that you will need regardless of what business you start is a website. It is important to build your online infrastructure up before you launch and have everything in place to successfully bring your product to market.

In today's age it is essential to have a website, even if you are not necessarily selling your product through a website of its own.

In a sense, your website and web infrastructure provider are another supplier. You pay them in exchange for a good or service of keeping your website online 24/7/365 with zero downtime. It is essential that you research a vendor that will be able to provide not only the best quality service for you but be quick to resolve any other issues as they arise.

*Figure 43: Choosing the right domain name is very important!*

# Your Domain Name

Your domain name is not something to be chosen lightly. Your domain name is your front line in your branding campaign for your online business (or your offline business's online presence). It is the name of your business—What people see when they want to go to your website. Careful consideration needs to go into choosing just the right domain name to represent your business. The following are some key points to consider:

### The Right Extension for the Right Site

Each type of site you want domain hosting for may serve a different market. Make sure the extension you use — .com, .net, .org, .biz, etc. — is the right extension for your market. If you are a business, get a .com domain if it is available for your desired name. If you are a non-profit organization, consider .org. If you are building a personal website and are on a budget, consider .us or some of the other lesser-known extensions. When in doubt, however, go for .com. The part of a URL people most often first forget is the extension. And when they're in doubt, .com is what they type in: .biz and .net should only be considered if you're completely attached to a particular name and the .com variant isn't available. My best suggestion for that scenario is to vary the domain hosting name and get the .com extension.

## The Shorter the Better

When picking domain names for your website, consider that people have to remember it to visit it. Not everyone is going to get to your website by clicking on a listing or an ad or a reciprocal link. Word of mouth leads increase when your domain hosting site's name is short and sweet. People also make fewer spelling mistakes and typos when trying to type in your URL directly.

## Stay Away from What Does not Belong to You

Big companies with trademarked names seem like tempting targets for domain names that generate loads of free (albeit unintentional) traffic. Heck, you could even sell the domain name back to them for a hefty sum. More than likely, however, you will just get sued. And chances are, if you are reading this book, they have better lawyers than you.

## The More the Merrier

Admittedly this catchy tag line is a little misleading. Considering registering a group of domain names in order to cover yourself for the inevitably of interested visitors typing in the wrong URL is an excellent idea. Try, if possible, to get the .com and .net variant of your domain name, or a variant with hyphens as well as the one without (always go for without hyphens first). But do not buy more than you can afford or more than you need. Once you own the domain hosting names, whatever they are and of whatever number, you still have to get people to visit them.

**Avoiding Incompleteness**

You cannot use symbols nor spaces in your domain name, so you will need to make sure that your domain name is memorable without spaces or symbols. Additionally, domain names are not case sensitive. So don't waste your time on that front.

Have you ever heard the concept that if you have an idea then someone else somewhere else in the world is having or has had the same idea before? Well, that is certainly the case with domain names, which is why you need to make all due haste in nabbing your ideal domain name. Otherwise, you may wind up compromising with an alternate far inferior name that does not accurately represent you or your company.

*Figure 44: Your hosting provider has racks upon racks of servers running the internet!*

# Your Hosting Provider

There are a lot of hosting companies out there, and generally they are all the same—But through my experience, I have found that there are a few ESSENTIAL services that a web host needs to offer to work with eCommerce and online businesses.

## cPanel Web Hosting

The cPanel web hosting control panel was produced by an organization with a similar name, and it was composed principally in the programming language "Perl". In spite of the fact that your feeling of utilizing cPanel will rely upon your own inclinations and desires, numerous trust that cPanel is a powerful and customizable website administration area which has effectively held up to the trial of time.

With the panel, you can control email addresses, databases, and domain names. With cPanel, all the hosted services are in one place. It has a very active community and has been constantly updated since its inception, making it the greatest customizable control panel on the market. The panel is developed in a way that it is easy to overcome any problems and difficulties that may occur while in use. It does not comprise of an advanced collection of features only; it has more features that makes it easy for all users regardless of your level of understanding.

## Usability

cPanel very easy to use. It is made in such a way that can be comprehended easily by anybody using it for the first time. The panel also comes with great features for professional users (multi-server management and IPv6 support just to name a few). It has very easy to use interface and it gives you the power to manage your site with no struggle.

## Reliability

At last, regardless of whether you have to move your cPanel website over to another hosting provider, you should rest guaranteed that cPanel will keep on offering a fabulous client relationship for a considerable length of time to come. Since there are many built in export and import tools, it is incredibly easy to transfer over to a new host when the time comes.

With such huge numbers of points of interest with running cPanel, it is not difficult to see why this control panel has stayed to be such a prominent platform for shared hosting clients throughout the decades. While different panels have come and gone, cPanel stays as solid as ever.

## Hosting Resources

You can easily observe your present asset use like transfer bandwidth, disk space, the number Email accounts, databases, sent messages, and so forth. Some hosting suppliers even set up email-based warnings on the off chance that you are near your hosting plan quota, so you can update your services without risking interrupted service.

## Extensibility

The features of cPanel can be broadened by utilizing outsider modules. One of those modules is the Softaculous auto installer which allows you to install numerous popular softwares to your website in a matter of seconds like WordPress, a popular blogging platform. There are also systems in place to secure your site or submit it to Google.

## Compatible with many Browsers

While other control panels are limited to certain browsers, cPanel works with all browsers. It is compatible with Chrome, Internet Explorer, Firefox, and Safari. This is what makes cPanel the best in the market since it will work perfectly well. Regardless of the digital set-up you use, it will still be compatible.

As it has been proven cPanel is a very is an exceptionally developed control that would be great for an online business. For our use case, it is essential to any site that runs any form of online business where people will be buying products and user data is stored.

## SSD Hosting

The solid-state drive is the most advanced storage medium out there, normally referred to as an SSD. Compared to a normal hard drive, there are no moving parts and therefore no delay in the time needed to access data in a certain part of the hard drive. Applied to web hosting, it supercharges the speed of data retrieval and site load speed. In an SSD data is stored in the microchip.

## Durability

The SSD keeps your data safe, even when you accidentally drop your laptop, or in the vibrations of a data center. The SSD has no moving parts. When, say, an earthquake occurs, nothing will interfere with the saved data--it still remains safe. The SSD depends on an embedded processor that does the reading and writing of data to a specific area on the disk rather than a spinning disk in the case of a normal hard disk drive. Normal drives are also much more fragile and volatile. The controller is very important as it decides at what speed the SSD operates on.

## Environmental Factors

An SSD can work in extraordinary high and low temperatures alongside its capacity to withstand outrageous stun and power. A snappy check of the specs of one of the current drives we looked into, the Corsair Force GT, demonstrates that it can work in temperatures from - 20 to 85 degrees Celsius, 90% dampness, and up to a height of 10,000 feet.

## Practically Indestructible

solid state drives a have been dropped from multistory structures, keep running after being run over by a car, utilized as hockey pucks while a player takes a slap-shot, and they have even been taped to the side of rockets just to demonstrate that they are as near indestructible as it gets.

## End Life Data Integrity

When a hard disk crashes, it has no use and all the stored information is destroyed because the processor that provides the key for where data is located on the disk is no longer available. The SSD does not crash. When it stops working, no information is lost. All stored data is saved. There is no research that has been able to tell for how long that information will be stored.

## Speed

Website load speed speaks to the most imperative part of why a hard drive is inferior to an SSD, especially for our needs on making our website quick and wide reaching. The SSD is about 90 times quicker than a normal hard disk drive. The main differences in speed arises from the way they are built:

- A hard drive asks for the data to which an arm should then float over the magnetically charged disk containing information. The disk turns at around 67mph. When it finds the data, it must lift it up from the disk and transmit the data back to the processor. Due to the mechanical nature of the beast, there is a slight delay in retrieving the data.
- An SSD works like oil traveling through a pipeline, where all is moved in and out. Data comes in, it is instantly found, and then put out the other end. Truth be told, on the grounds that the run of the mill SSD works on eight channels (or ways to the controller), it is like eight pipelines coming back with the data replying to one 'pipe' input.

In terms of making sure that your website is online as well as quick, there is nothing better than SSD web hosting.

## SSL Encryption

How can we process transactions securely on the web? Any safe transaction should happen between the customer and the web site in a manner that no one can read or intercept the transaction details. To enable this fast transaction, SSL encryption, otherwise called as secure sockets layer encryption is very useful. This protocol works through the encryption routines and programs that are found on the web host and browser.

Once you know the basic meaning and facts related to SSL encryption, you can activate the SSL option through your web host and provide necessary information to your clients in a secure environment.

When a site uses no encryption, anyone can see the data that is being transmitted between your computer and your website. It is basically like walking around in public with a sign that has your credit card number on it. If anyone wants it, the data is there for the taking. Any hacker using his brains and tools can break the security of the website easily.

With SSL encryption, it is as though you go out in public with your credit card number written on a poster in a secret language that only you and your friend you are buying something from have the dictionary for.

In this way, you are keeping your website secure and prevent others from snooping in on what data you are passing back and forth on your website.

If your website deals with payments, collects personal data like emails, birthdays, or other bank or credit card details, then a high level of encryption should be maintained to gain goodwill and trust among customers. They will feel safe and comfortable working with you and will be also feel safe about the details they have shared. Additionally, SSL certificates work with almost all browsers.

*Figure 45: You can create your website yourself or hire someone to do it for you!*

# Creating your Website

I will take this quick opportunity to talk about my venture, Fitzgerald Tech Solutions (fitzgeraldtechsolutions.com). As an organization, we thrive on helping you set up your new venture. We design solutions that help small and budding business take full advantage of the opportunities that are made possible by the new internet era. We will partner you not only in building and maintain your digital assets, we will also create the required social media assets and manage them for you. We will work closely with your team to generate the right returns from your investments.

In addition to that, we sell both web hosting and domain names and all of the features covered above come in all of our hosting packages.

Give us a shot if you are interested in keeping your site online!

# Building a Site

Let us start with deciding whether to utilize a platform, e-commerce marketplace or build your own e-commerce site.

An e-commerce website is the most immediate type of online business you can begin, contrasted with a business that utilizes third-person commercial centers like, eBay Etsy, Airbnb, or Amazon.

When you build and host your own e-commerce site, you will be selling your goods and services directly to your customers, without a "go-between."

In some cases, this can be a good thing.

# Hosting your own website

By having your website hosted on a web hosting provider, you hold control. The best part about a direct internet business webpage (e-commerce) is the degree of control you have over your store. You will have the option to redo basically every part of your web-based business, including the look and feel of your store. Be that as it may, this adaptability can make the way toward beginning increasingly complicated with different issues on the website as well.

Concentrate on the client's experience. Your greatest concerns about making sure your user has a memorable and easy experience will allow you to be different in the industry. Picking the correct website layout is necessary, as is ensuring that your shopping cart programming is appropriate for your business. Make certain to look at the different shopping cart alternatives accessible—from OpenCart to X-Cart and some more.

## Using a marketplace

There are increasingly more third-party web based commercial hubs accessible, such as Amazon, eBay, Etsy, and even Airbnb or Fiverr, contingent upon your item or service. Building a business using these web-based business commercial centers can be less difficult, since you'll need to settle on less choices, and you won't need to fabricate your site yourself—you'll utilize a current format.

In any case, you will definitely pay to utilize that third party. A few destinations charge by the quantity of item postings you utilize every month, and others, like Airbnb, charge you an assistance expense when you get a booking.

Assess the upsides and downsides. The way that your clients should visit the third party to purchase from you has advantages and disadvantages. If you find it vital to lease your property, utilizing Airbnb's foundation implies that it will likely be simpler for anybody to discover you when they scan for housing in your general vicinity due to Airbnb's developing prevalence.

But on the other hand, it is simpler for customers to think about comparable items, which makes your capacity to separate yourself increasingly significant. For example, on the off chance that you choose to utilize Etsy to sell handmade cutting boards, however, when a prospective client scans for cutting boards on the site, they'll pass through possibly hundreds or thousands of moderately comparative postings or listings.

Concentrate on what makes you stick out. In case you're utilizing an e-commerce site, give specific consideration to the nature of the pictures you use on your page. Good product photography can separate your posting. But remember, hosting your own e-commerce site is not a free pass for using mediocre images either. Either way, customers will rely on images to form an opinion about your product or service's value.

Select the appropriate platform. Pay attention to whether the marketplace you are considering attracts people in your target demographic. The initial customer personas that were created will come in handy at this point.

However, remember that there is not generally one marketplace that works for each area of business. Set aside the effort to investigate the best one for you. In case you are selling workmanship or custom artwork, search for a site that is utilized by different specialists in the same industry. In case you are selling old comic books, search for a site that draws in loads of customers hoping to purchase utilized comic books. Furthermore, read the fine print. Make sure you know what you are getting into before you pull the trigger on a specific platform.

# Setting up Our Site

In this section, I will be talking a tad about the process of actually getting your site set up and launched and some of the tips and tricks I have learned from years of experience in this field.

## Choose a Name

Deciding on your business name and registering your domain name should be done in tandem. The last thing you want is to find out that one or the other (the domain you bought or the name you chose) is registered to some other business.

There are clear benefits to having a domain name that is the same as your company or product name. You want to make it as easy as possible for people to find you when they search for you online. The same is true when you are naming your storefront if you're using an online platform like Etsy or eBay.

Even if you wind up using a third party to actually sell your good, I highly recommend still registering the domain name for your company and setting up an informational site that links to your store, wherever it may be.

## Build out your site

In some instances, it will definitely make sense to build your own site. If you are building an actual online product, like a software as a service product, your team probably already has the skills necessary to build your marketing website.

If you're simply using the web as a platform to sell something analog (clothing or a subscription meal box, for example, or a service like consulting, design services, or even vacation rentals) you might benefit more from using an existing platform, or at least a templated e-commerce option, so you're not starting from scratch.

Hiring a web design firm, like Fitzgerald Tech Solutions, is always an option. Either way, remember that it is never a bad idea to build out a minimum viable product (MVP) site first. Meaning, you do not have to build a 100 percent perfect site right out of the gate. Test your hypothesis that your product or service is marketable using a lower cost, simpler option at first. From there, you can gain feedback and make all of the changes necessary to make your site or product exactly what people want to see.

## Make it mobile friendly

It is still possible to build websites and elect to use templates that aren't mobile friendly. You can pretty much broadly assume that it is a bad idea. However, you decide to build your online presence, do not skip making it mobile friendly.

If your site is not optimized for mobile, your users will have a less positive experience when they try to find you from their phones, but Google will also penalize you in search results, meaning you'll be harder for new customers to find organically.

## Pay attention to image quality

Poorly lit or sloppily composed images on your site do not do anything to build your credibility. Whether you are selling products, ideas, or experiences, using high-quality images will make a difference.

If you are selling products, either hire a freelancer to do the job right or invest in the equipment that you'll need to take and edit high-quality photos. If you are not sure you can afford professional images, check with local colleges to see if there are students looking to learn and build their portfolios that cost less than well-established professionals.

And do not fall into the trap of settling for terrible stock photos. You know the ones. The super corporate looking or 1997-esque images will not be doing you any favors, especially if you're entering a more crowded market.

## Think about blogging

Content marketing (blogging) may or may not be part of your initial marketing plan. The key here is to retain optionality. If you are building your site from scratch or using an e-commerce template, make sure to build the site in such a way that adding a blog wouldn't be a major reconstruction.

## Consider monetization and affiliate partnerships

Monetizing your e-commerce site through affiliate partnership and on-site ads is something to consider.

If you do decide to incorporate third-party ads on your site, start slowly, especially if your site is minimalist at first. You do not want prospective customers to be confused about what you're actually trying to sell on your site or overwhelmed by intrusive ads.

## Do not set it and forget it

When you launch your site, if it is self-hosted, set up analytics systems to monitor site traffic, or look into whether your third-party solution can offer you monthly insights on how well your site is performing. Use that data to test small changes to your site that might have an impact on your sales.

You will also have to pay attention to things like choosing the right shopping cart, payment methods, inventory and order management, accounting integration.

# Additional Information

A lot of what you require can be found online. It is good to do a lot of research to be well prepared once it is time to make investment decisions. Most of these decisions will establish your success or failure in either product quality terms or in monitory terms, so be very careful before making these calls. Some of the available literature we like, and you can use is as follows:

- https://www.thebalance.com/how-to-find-a-wholesale-distributor-2531713
- https://www.entrepreneur.com/article/66028
- https://www.shopify.com/blog/13975985-how-to-find-a-manufacturer-or-supplier-for-your-product-idea
- https://mywifequitherjob.com/the-best-way-to-find-vendors-for-your-online-store/
- https://www.businessknowhow.com/startup/findsuppliers.htm

- https://www.sba.gov/blogs/4-tips-researching-and-finding-wholesale-suppliers

- https://www.entrepreneur.com/article/175242

- https://www.shopify.com/blog/14327905-countdown-to-launching-your-ecommerce-business

- https://www.shopify.com/blog/14459769-ecommerce-business-blueprint-how-to-build-launch-and-grow-a-profitable-online-store

- http://mashable.com/2013/09/30/launch-online-business/#iZQVXA6cEiq0

- https://articles.bplans.com/steps-to-starting-an-online-business/

- https://us.businessesforsale.com/us/search/technology-and-media-businesses-for-sale/articles/12-ways-to-launch-a-successful-online-business

- https://www.bigcommerce.com/blog/how-to-start-online-business/

- https://suitcaseentrepreneur.com/build-online-business-even-no-idea/

- https://www.paypal.com/us/webapps/mpp/brc/how-to-launch-your-online-business

- https://www.forbes.com/sites/johnrampton/2016/01/26/6-myths-about-launching-a-successful-online-business/#4d4afe4913D5

# 9 TO THE MOON—THE BUSINESS LAUNCH

This is how it all comes together – T minus 10 to launch!

To be successful in business, you will require an efficient supply of things, people, and services working on your side.

We have done a lot by now, just to put things together we have covered:

- Building our core business idea around a strong skill that we have
- Improving our skill set by identifying additional skills needed for success
- Building the right kind of machine (computer) for our online business

- Validating the core idea to ensure right way forward
- Researching the market for inputs and course corrections
- Interacting with customers to get a final feel for our product/service
- Documented our business canvas/business plan / legal entity / legal document
- Establish the required team
- Contracted the suppliers

The project is now **ready for launch**! This is the big-ticket item – decisions for the following questions will be required to take our business online:

- How do I charge the customer?

  _____
  _____
  _____
  _____
  _____

- How do I manage orders?

  _____
  _____
  _____
  _____
  _____

- How do I manage invoicing and payments on the website?

  _____
  _____
  _____
  _____

—  How do I interact with potential customers?

_____

_____

_____

_____

_____

—  How do I build an ever-growing list of interested partners?

_____

_____

_____

_____

_____

—  How do I make the site engaging?

_____

_____

_____

_____

_____

—  How do I promote the launch?

_____

_____

_____

_____

_____

The direct analogy of an online store is to a physical store is very helpful here. If we have not decided to build an e-commerce site, we would have to build a physical store. The only difference is that a physical store is limited by location and opening time for its clients, whereas the online store is open 24/7 and can cater to customers from across the world.

# Launching

Now that you have the site ready, it is time to plan a launch. Regarding our customer personas, we will be able to target the exact emotions, thoughts, and needs of our customer's visit. It is a good starting point to do some advertising and announcing our launch. The website or platform we use will also be the main tool to build some visibility. We should plan an on the ground and social media engagement plan for announcing our launch. A very good idea is to arrange for guest posts in relevant blogs to make more people regardless of their position aware of our presence in the market. Additionally, social media blasts are very helpful for getting the word out there.

# Do not rush launching your site

With immediate access to millions of potential customers, it is tempting to launch your site as soon as you can, regardless of what it looks like or where you are in the development phase of your e-commerce business.

If you want to stay ahead of your e-commerce competition, be sure to do the following before you launch.

—   Have a solid marketing strategy that includes consistent branded messaging and omnichannel experiences across online platforms that your customers already frequent.

—   Determine your average customer's entire path and timeline with steps you expect them to take along the way. The path starts with how they will encounter your brand online and ends with how and when they will receive their products.

- Know how customers will reach you with complaints or concerns and how you will handle them. Knowing how people could reach you could make or break your online reputation in the beginning.

- Verify that the speed of your e-commerce platform is up to par with what your customers expect and are accustomed to on other sites. Also, ensure that your site is easily accessible and responsive on mobile devices.

- Choose which analytical tools you will use to monitor user history, purchase history, feedback, and other customer data so that you can adapt to it as quickly as possible.

## The Launch Plan

Since every business is different, there is no one clear cut way to launch a site. The two main things you will want to take into account are:

1. Gaining Hype
2. The Release

*Figure 46: Good hype is essential to a successful launch*

## Gaining Hype

One of the harder things to do when you are ready to launch your new venture is to gain the initial hype over your new product. This is with good reason too, since the product you are making does not exist in the eyes of your customers yet. One way that you can gain the initial hype over your launch is leaving it vague and using mystery to hide what it is you are doing. That is what I did when I launched Fitzgerald Tech Solutions. I set up a landing page with an email list form and alerted all of my social media channels that I had a big announcement coming soon and gave an exact time and date. I then kept giving smaller and smaller hints as time progressed. I even had a countdown timer until when I would deliver the big news.

While this tactic worked for me, you will have to judge your target market and see what they would be most attentive to and how you can most effectively reach the biggest size target demographic you can. It is important to actually spend the money on advertising your services once they have been launched rather than building up hype, so hold off on placing any ads right now.

In the next section, I will describe how I released FTS and how I was able to have a successful launch.

*Figure 47: You did it!*

## The Release

Once the time comes for you to deliver the news of your new business and the launch, come out guns a 'blazin! Post a short description of what you are doing to all of your social media channels, update your LinkedIn, email all of your subscribers, post in forums, hand out flyers, and drive sales.

When I launched Fitzgerald Tech Solutions, it was easy for me to tap into my loyal following on social media. They were more than happy to share my post with their friends and encourage likes on my Facebook page and visits to my site.

When you launch your venture, be sure to let people know about exactly what you do, and how you can easily order their services. Another interesting tactic would be to do a giveaway on your launch.

You can offer up the lowest-end product to a lucky winner who says shares your page or likes a post.

Before you know it, you will be engulfed in orders from your new venture! In the next chapter, I tackle the challenges of running the business and detail how to stay alive as your business gets its first few customers.

# Writing a good flyer

To make our sales pop, I will detail a bit on how to write a good sales letter, or flyer, for your business. It is actually simpler and easier to make a good flyer than most people think. And to make one, all you need is patience and the willingness to learn.

A good flyer has an attention grabbing headline. The headline is often the basis of most readers' first impressions of a flyer, and you know how first impressions last, don't you? If they don't like what your headline says – or worse, if they're absolutely uninterested in what your headline is broadcasting – then they'll not only dump your flyer in the trash, but they'll also indicate any forthcoming online mail from you as spam.

An effective headline is short but direct to the point. It tells readers not only what they can expect from the rest of the flyer but also how they can benefit it.

## A Good Flyer is Always about the Reader.

A good flyer always acknowledges the fact that the business owes everything to its customers. It does not ramble on about how great its profit margins are but humbly admits that it owes its success to its loyal customers.

And when selling something, a good flyer always focuses on what the reader would get from the product. If you're selling roses, for instance, you don't waste too much time waxing poetry about how beautiful roses are, but you focus more on how customers would benefit from having flowers at home, rose baths, aromatherapy from roses and so forth.

## A Good Flyer is Rarely More than One Page Long.

Everyone is living on borrowed time, and more and more people are becoming aware of this. If you have got a really great offer to make, that's good…but it wouldn't make people change their minds about what they deem appropriate or inappropriate to allocate their time for. And more often than not, flyers are filed under the "not more than one-page" category. Anything longer than that, and readers might feel too lazy to continue reading.

And while we are on the subject of writing guidelines, make sure that your flyer also consists of some short paragraphs instead of a few but long paragraphs. Unless you are writing something incredibly shocking or titillating, it's highly probable that only a few people would have the patience and interest to forge on.

## A Good Flyer has an Attention-Grabbing Postscript.

 No, it does not mean that you have to deliberately forget to include something in the body of your flyer, but a postscript can be used to reiterate or emphasize one of the main points of your flyer.

Case studies have shown that people often read the headlines and postscripts of letters first then use it as the basis for deciding whether or not to continue reading the rest of the letter. Take advantage of this by making sure you have got something interesting to say in your postscript. It can be a repeated invitation or a declaration about the promo period and the need to act NOW.

## A Good Flyer Does Not Take "No" for an Answer.

All flyers end with a strong call for action, or simply put, strong words of encouragement to purchase the product or service on offer.

But a good flyer also considers the chance that the customer may be interested but not yet fully prepared to buy. In this case, he also includes a very persuasively worded invitation to call in order to know more about what's offer. The letter clinches the deal by offering an incentive if the customer simply asks for additional information.

## A Good Flyer is Also Visually Attractive.

A customer will feel more inclined to read a flyer if it looks pretty to the eye – no matter if great style and graphics have nothing to do with content. Consider this: if you have two books talking about the same topic, which would you choose – the one with ugly or beautiful cover and text? If you aren't good at this part, have a graphic designer take a look at the design for you and you will be satisfied with the results!

## A Good Flyer is a Product of Extensive Tests.

When you have proofread your flyer for the last time, do not press the send button just yet. Test it first with sample readers. If they like it, great! But if they do not then take careful note of what they are saying and revise.

By following some of these tips, you can write a flyer that surely will help you generate leads.

# Gaining leads

While companies everywhere are struggling to find qualified leads for their business, many overlook the obvious. There are ways of generating leads with little or no cost that will not detract from or interfere with family relations or friendships. They can also almost guarantee that people that are added to your network are interested in your business, bringing a new level of quality to your lead generation.

One of the most commonly used methods of generating leads is through the use of online press releases. When a public relations company includes a write up about your business, it adds credibility to what you are saying and selling much more than a paid advertisement. People see the inclusion of a press release as having the backing of the publisher of the public relations network and therefore must be a legitimate business.

You will have to remember the basic rules of writing press releases in order to write an effective one. The content has to be newsworthy and not a blatant attempt at self-promotion to be considered for inclusion in online and offline publications. New products, new business methods, and even personnel promotions can help a press release see the light of print or a PR firm's website.

There are also article distribution services you can use to get the word out about your company and its products. These companies allow individuals to post articles, usually for free, for distribution through online magazines geared towards the interests of their readers. Writing and distributing articles containing useful information may get it published in a third-party publication. When people see your name in many different publications on the same subject, they will begin to view you as an expert in that field.

Every published article from a distribution service will contain a little something about you as well as the address of your business. The people who like what they read and want to know more will visit your site because they have a real interest in what you do or what you sell, almost instantly becoming a member of your lead network.

Keeping an updated blog is one of the big trends going on today. Other than personal and social network sites, starting a blog about the industry in which your business is a part can also bring more people to your network. You have to careful not to make a blog an obvious advertisement by talking about the benefits of certain types of products and not necessarily the ones you sell. Include your internet address in every published blog and invite others to post comments on the subjects as well as visit your own website without selling directly.

By doing a lot of the fishing for leads on your own, using your own efforts, and not paying for leads of questionable origins, you can quickly add to your lead base and begin to realize significant increases in traffic to your site. If you lack the time and talent to write your own articles or blog entries, you can hire a freelance writer to ghostwrite them for you, still saving money on the price of buying leads.

## Leads from clients

The best sales leads often come from your customers. Having customers give you a list of prospective leads for new business that they know for you is direct marketing at its best. To make this request, you have to consider what you are asking the customer for carefully. To get a loyal customer to help you is not that difficult, but they are doing a lot for you, and you should reward them for that.

Finding business is a quest for new accounts and more clients. Even small tidbits of information from current clients can help tip you off to opportunities to reach out and market to a specific lead in a more effective way. The cost is nothing more than subtle shifts in thought and marketing strategy. You never market and attempt to sell to someone without knowing their needs. If the client is another business owner, the best way to market this is to address their needs directly and effectively. By learning what their business needs are, you can understand where your product or service will help them.

By making selling a personal experience for you and the customer, it is easy to look for more connections immediately. By increasingly understanding your leads, their needs, and how to fill them, you are optimizing your sales process. The thing to remember is that your customers are the best sales lead generator.

How do you ask for sales leads? Perhaps casually, but showing you appreciate all of the business current customers bring you. If you are trying to determine leads from another business owner, it may be a different approach than asking an individual. The way for you don't make a customer or business owner uncomfortable is to phase it in a way to make them realize that the recommended referral is a way for you to maintain the integrity of your business and there may be a reward in store for them bringing your business whether that would be a lower rate, more services, or a better service. As a business owner, you should prefer referrals because you trust your customers and want to maintain a business that deals with responsible businesses and individuals.

If the customer thinks highly of your product or service, then they usually are happy to oblige. Remember, the customer is working in conjunction with you to ensure that his friends or business associates are getting a good product or service. If you give your customers good service, they usually will gladly work at being your best sales lead generator. This is finding business the right way.

## The Psychology of a Seller

In order to understand how to appeal to our market the right way is understanding how they think, and make sure you as a seller understands that. A person's attitude has a lot more to do with the level of their success than one's aptitude, ability, IQ, education, or other factors do. I want to get into the details of a salesperson's psychology so that when it comes to building your team and individual team members, you are equipped with the knowledge of what is going up in that head of your customer As a business owner, you have already experienced being a salesperson yourself. However, it never hurts to review and be reminded of what it is like to "carry the bag." I also want to emphasize the mental game because so many companies focus on external things, like product knowledge, licensing, or other issues. And while these things are all important, companies that focus on such externalities often neglect the cultivation of their salespeople's proper mindset and do not fully understand how a potential customer would feel and what they are thinking. I have always found this selling mentality ironic because it's what's going on in the inside that will most dramatically affect sales.

A direct relationship exists between self-image and sales performance. If you do not already, try to get a handle on how you or your sales reps perceive themselves. What kind of self-talk plays in their brains all day long? You and your team will never experience exponential success if it is not something you can mentally conceive of first. The major precursor to envisioning success in the workplace is envisioning success in oneself and one's abilities. How can you, as a business owner, cultivate healthy, solid self-confidence and self-confidence in you and your employees? One of the easiest ways to do so is to offer sincere praise. Ralph Waldo Emerson said, "Every man is entitled to be valued by his best moments." There is no need to fear that you will create an egomaniac by giving someone simple but honest praise and appreciation for good, hard work.

Often, it is more effective to praise the specific act rather than the person. This way, your praise is attached to something distinct and concrete. Praise is harder to be interpreted as flattery or favoritism when there is a specific and concrete thing being praised. General compliments may produce a temporary effect, but they can incite jealousy in others and create even more insecurity in the recipient if the specific activity that merited the compliment remains unknown.

After unrooted praising, there is a new pressure to live up to this higher standard, even though the praised individual is not sure how they get it. Even more insecurity is bred if the praised individual fears you will retract your praise. That is because in not knowing concretely how they earned it, they don't know how to keep it. One single person feeling this kind of anxiety or insecurity can really cause your entire team building effort to backfire. Have you ever witnessed or experienced coworkers who huddled together to complain after a "pep rally" or meeting with the boss? Instead of feeling inspired and motivated, all they could do was gripe. Unfortunately, it only takes one person's bad attitude to drag down the rest.

We know that when a specific behavior is praised, that behavior will increase. At a small college in Virginia, 24 students in a psychology course decided to see whether they could use compliments to change the way women on campus dressed. For a while, they complimented all the female students who were wearing blue. The percentage of the female student population wearing blue then rose from 25 percent to 38 percent. The researchers then switched to complimenting any woman who wore red. This shift in the color being praised caused the appearance of red on campus to double from 11 percent to 22 percent. Praise is a simple but often overlooked concept. If you want to use this technique to your best advantage, be sure you give honest and sincere praise.

Closely related to praise is acceptance. We all long for acceptance. We want to feel like our actions and contributions help an effort or cause. We all want to be noticed by others. We also all want to be someone of significance who is held in high regard. Knowledge of this common craving from acceptance can help you motivate your team. If you can make them feel that their help is appreciated, that they are personally accepted, and that their contributions are essential, they will be more inspired to perform.

When your team members feel accepted unconditionally, with no strings attached, their doubts, fears, and inadequacies will go out the window. One way to make your team feel accepted is to offer them genuine thanks. Seek to make a conscientious and deliberate effort to thank people in all aspects of your professional life. Do not assume your team members know you care about and appreciate them. Do not make the mistake of thinking that a paycheck is thanks enough. One of the main reasons why people are dissatisfied with their sales job is because they are never thanked or given any recognition for their efforts.

Often, individuals increase their feelings of acceptance by building their association with certain people, places, or things. This sense of identification has been referred to as the Social Identity Theory. For example, a sports fan may enhance his sense of belonging by plastering his walls with his favorite team's sports paraphernalia. Even though no one on that team has any clue who he is, he feels better about himself, just because of the association and identity he has created for himself with that team.

Are there ways in which you can use the Social Identity Theory to your advantage? Think of ways to create a strong team association. These methods should be things that are unique to the team, and that helps team members individually feel like they are "insiders." Maybe your team needs a mascot, a mission statement, or even a theme song. I once knew a sales team that played the theme music from Rocky over the loudspeaker every time someone closed a sale. Things like this might seem silly, but they build team spirit and morale. If you worry that things like this will be distracting or disruptive to your particular workplace, look for ways to adapt. The energy that grows from each team member feeling accepted is worth the effort.

Throughout this chapter, we have detailed the many ways in which you are able to utilize methods to launch your business successfully and get those first few sales. Another great thing to consider is you should already have your first set of clients from feasibility studies mentioned earlier in this book! Talk to them and make sure that they are still interested in the product and want to support your new venture. This will allow you to be able to gain some awesome loyal clients and work with them in the future to help your business grow.

These are the ground-floor clients. These are the people that have trusted you to make the idea a reality. Treat them well and they will refer you more business!

Now that we have a launched and successful business, we will talk about keeping everything balanced.

# 10 KEEPING YOURSELF ALIVE— CONTINUED INVOLVEMENT

Engaging with your audience – building a product pipeline

Once we have successfully navigated the launch, the focus shifts from building the business to sustaining the business and growing it. Everyone likes to talk about the fancy start-up as that is the most exciting phase of a new business, once launched the excitement is over, and we now must grapple with the daily grind. In most cases this isn't the case because now that we have the flow of cash, we can use that to grow our business even more! We need to look for customers and understand the changes in the marketplace that will impact our business. Additionally, we must engage with the existing customers, build loyalty, resolve quality issues, and ensure legal compliance. The time after the launch is like a mid-life crisis, motivation levels are down, and no one is looking for you, you are all on your own.

*Figure 48: Make sure you stay current and relevant in the changing markets*

This is when some things done well before your launch will help not only to keep things in shape but also grow the business. The basics are to be driven in this stage, and the very simple truth about an online business is to keep engaging with the audience. We must ensure that we stay competitive, build an engaging blog, and do proper Search Engine Optimization (or SEO) to ensure customers can find us when they are looking for us. This is the time to push our way forward in the market and to focus on engagement with current customers and building credible SEO optimization so we can be found easily. Let us start with some focus on staying competitive. We particularly like the approach detailed by blueswitch.com, the 5 points they highlight are as follows:

## Establish a Niche

It is not always a good idea to sell everything you can in the world of e-commerce businesses. Small to medium-sized businesses that participate in niche markets online have more engaged and loyal customers than their competitors. They create niches, or specialized markets, based on their audience's interests, fears, aspirations, lifestyles, and needs. As we highlighted earlier, creating a niche is essential to figuring out your target market. The thing is now that you are in the niche, refine your lineup based on what you have observed in your target market. These are the same things we worked on while deciding the skill around which we will build our business, and this is well captured in our customer personas.

For instance, if you sell skin-care products that have the same ingredients and benefits as your e-commerce competition, it can be difficult to stand out from all the rest. However, if you offer products made of ingredients with unique health benefits, such as organic ingredients, it will be easier for you to create a demand for your specialty product. You will weed out the competition that only offers chemically based products that don't provide a unique health benefit. Please refer to our discussion on finding differentiators for our business. This is how they will help.

## The Human Factor of Business

Especially as online technically skilled people, we seem to want to automate everything, including client interaction. One of the biggest things I have learned through creating businesses and client relationships is the beauty of personalized service. People generally want to be treated well, and by providing personalized service or giving a check-in call every once in a while, this simple act can allow you to go that extra mile where you can out serve the competition. This way you can make sure that your customers stay with you and remain happy. It can even lead to discussions on innovating the services or creating new products or services to make more income. Personal service goes a long way!

Another factor to consider is the skills that you have. (see what I did there!) If you aren't good at communicating what your customers want to hear at a level they can understand, it may be beneficial to potentially contract with a marketing or client interaction team to make sure that the client experience is great.

## Shape the client experience

How do you want the client to feel when they use your product or service? What emotions do you want someone to feel when they think of your company, product, or service? By understanding how you want the clients to feel, you can work towards making sure that these emotions are felt by the marketing materials, purchase and onboarding process, and potentially product packaging/framing.

*Figure 49: Making your clients happy is the core to sustaining and growing your business.*

## Building Client Trust

Clients work with professionals they trust. Building trust is an ongoing process. Here are 10 ways to build trust with both old and new clients.

## Keep your agreements with your clients

If you promise delivery on a particular day, make sure to deliver when it was promised. Even something as small as the time you have scheduled an appointment is an agreement. Each time you break an agreement with a client, you break their trust. One way to mitigate the damages from this broken trust is to communicate well in advance any changes to promises.

## Create realistic client expectations

Help the client to understand exactly what you will do for him or her or how the product will help better their life. Put boundaries around what is included in your service and what is not. What will create extra charges? How and when will you be billing the client? Living up to the expectations you create helps your clients to take you at your word.

## Help the client to understand the process

If your client understands how you and your office works, the client can then know what to expect and when to expect it.

## Explain your plan and strategy

Not only does the client need to understand the way you and your company work but also what the plan and strategy is place for them in the future if you are offering them a service. This will help client to know what to expect and when to expect it. Trust comes when the client feels confident and comfortable with the plan and the strategy.

## Never over promise

It is tempting to promise whatever the client requests without consulting a schedule or asking if it is doable. Over promising often causes broken agreements and thus broken trust.

## Carefully explain the client's role

When a client is clear on what their role is, then the client gets clear on what progress can be made without his or her involvement and what needs his or her input before moving on. Getting really clear on what the client needs to do to move his or her case forward, helps you work as a team and builds trust.

## Discuss potential pitfalls

Nothing disturbs the trust of a client more than when something unexpected happens. (If it is good, of course you can celebrate! WooHoo!) Guard against something negative happening as a surprise by discussing the potential pitfalls with the client.

## Review the agreement in detail

Any agreements that the client is going to have to make should be discussed in detail. Trust is built over a long period of time, but it can be broken easily. A surprise that results from an agreement the client made but is unaware of breaks that trust quickly.

## Avoid making the client feel stupid

No one likes to feel stupid. If clients feel that you think they are stupid they will no longer entrust you with their ideas or thoughts. Clients who do not feel valued by the professional may stop trusting that person. Professionals probably do not set out to make a client feel stupid. In fact, it may be an attitude, an inadvertent comment, or a look that gives the client that impression. Be aware of your inner thoughts. They show up without your noticing. Use careful language. Think before you speak.

# Do not allow interruptions at meetings

If you take interruptions, such as a phone call, or answering emails when you are with a client, it makes them feel they are not important to you. Eventually you erode the good will and trust that you had with them.

When you build trust with your consumers, the next part comes naturally, they develop brand loyalty.

## Instill brand loyalty

You can instill brand loyalty with your prospects and existing customers online by engaging with them through a blog and social media content. Find your unique voice and value proposition as an e-commerce business, solve a specific problem, or enhance the lives of your audience in some way. Do this without trying to sell them something every time you share a post.

Additionally, give your existing customers what they want to secure their loyalty with you instead of with your e-commerce competitors. If you receive repeated requests for free shipping, for example, then give it to them. Even if you only offer free shipping on promotional items or for limited time periods, they will notice when you give them what they want, and they will likely buy more and share their experiences with others.

## Strategize your Pricing

It is easy to only focus on getting new customers when you run an e-commerce business, but you should invest in retention strategies for high-value customers too. Implement loyalty programs or bonuses for your best customers. They will be reluctant to switch brands once they have accumulated a certain amount of rewards points because they don't want to lose out on special offers or discounts they've earned.

When setting prices, keep in mind that you do not always have to have the lowest price either. Customers buy for many reasons. While price is commonly one of those reasons, you should not compete exclusively on price. A good point to remember in order to stay ahead of e-commerce competition is that customers are willing to pay more for things such as higher-quality products and better customer service.

## Stay educated and ahead of trends

Always be aware of new technologies and trends that have relevance to your e-commerce business and know which ones your competitors are using. Customers expect e-commerce sites that load quickly and are intuitive to use. If they cannot navigate your site because of outdated technology, then they certainly won't feel comfortable inputting their credit card information.

If you stay educated and ahead of trends in e-commerce, you will be aware of the best ways to enhance your e-commerce platform, market it effectively, and build loyal customers who trust your brand. This will keep you ahead of the e-commerce competition.

## Additional Information

Lots of learning is required in this area and as expected the net is full of inputs for you. Some of the good ones, the one I liked are:

- https://www.boostability.com/how-small-businesses-can-stay-competitive-top-2017-digital-marketing-trends
- http://www.sbmarketingtools.com/5-website-updates-for-businesses-to-stay-competitive-online/
- https://www.marketingdonut.co.uk/marketing-strategy/ten-ways-to-keep-ahead-of-the-competition
- https://www.inc.com/molly-reynolds/5-ways-to-create-a-highly-competitive-e-commerce-business.html
- https://www.inc.com/nina-ojeda/2-key-ways-to-stay-competitive-online.html
- https://www.entrepreneur.com/article/287450

- https://www.allbusiness.com/5-strategies-physical-stores-to-stay-competitive-in-online-retail-world-110627-1.html
- https://www.blueswitch.com/5-ways-stay-competitive-world-ecommerce-business/

# Building good SEO

Now that we have a good idea of how to stay competitive, we need to work on staying connected with the customer. We need a good strategy to engage with customers. This can be done with a content marketing strategy and some good old SEO on the website. This is a large and continually evolving world. It makes sense to stay updated with what search engines like google give out as guidelines. But a few basics are as follows:

Just as wheels without an engine leaves us pedaling, content without an SEO strategy cannot keep up in a digital marketplace. And just like an engine with no wheels, SEO without content is a shiny machine that goes nowhere. Content needs SEO to stand out in the din of mediocre blog posts clogging up the internet these days, and Google has said that one of the top three ranking factors for organic search is "content."

But what does that mean? Not any content, surely. Unfortunately, search engines are not handing out checklists for "high-quality content," and they probably never will. That means it's up to those of us who geek out on this kind of thing to study search results, mine Google Analytics and create massive spreadsheets that we pretend to be bored by but secretly love — all to bring you (and ourselves, who are we kidding?) a comprehensive guide to creating "high-quality" SEO content.

# SEO your content strategy

Too many marketers are still waiting until the end of content creation to bring in SEO as a promotional tool. They try to figure out what they have just created, so they can plug in a few keywords and links. But an effective content marketing strategy should start with a keyword and user intent research. Once you know what queries your audience is using, and what kind of content they are looking for, you can design a content strategy that answers their specific questions and helps move them through the funnel.

High-quality content:

- Is based on an understanding of your audience, as well as keyword and user intent research. Use your audience's language and provide the information they are actually looking for.
- Helps the reader complete one specific task. Long content (1,000+ words) tends to rank better in organic results, in part because it is thorough. That said, stay on task and do not let the content lose focus.
- Features an enticing call to action or a clear next step. When you know your readers and their buyer journeys, your content can point them to more of what they want.

# Design good content

Good User Experience, or UX, is good SEO. When users are engaged, they consume more content, interact with it, and share it. From the overarching structure to the details of the layout, make sure you are designing good content.

There are plenty of philosophies about which characteristics make content "good" — or "sticky" or "thought leadership." They are all worthy considerations, and every piece of content should cover at least a few:

- Simple/Clear/Coherent

- Unexpected
- Concrete
- Credible/Valid/Experienced
- Emotional
- Entertaining
- Inspiring
- Educational
- Relevant
- Deep/Thorough
- Practical
- Novel/Unique (in value, not just in content)
- Trustworthy

And as you continue to design content, keep your audience in mind: you are writing for people, so search engines can also understand — not vice versa.

## High-quality content:

- Is written to its audience, not your peers. Make sure the language is neither too simple nor full of industry jargon.
- Is shareable. Take a step back and ask yourself if you would share it — and, if so, could you? (i.e., are social sharing buttons readily available?)
- Can be scanned quickly. Use short paragraphs, callouts, bold text, bullet points, numbered lists, quotes and so on to make the text easy on the eyes and easy to digest quickly.
- Uses strong titles and Headings. This creates enticing, actionable titles that use keywords strategically and naturally. CoSchedule has a nice headliner analyzer tool if you need help here.
- Features ideal results, common objections and/or time frames in sub headers. Anticipate the audience's hopes, fears, and concerns.

- Is better than current high-ranking pages. Spy out the competition. Review the pages that are currently ranking well for target keywords and ask yourself if your content is better. Make sure it is better.

## Create correct content

Is there anything as unsettling as a typo in an otherwise great piece of content? No. There is not. While there is no evidence, at this time, that grammar is a ranking signal, it's a UX/credibility concern. Additionally, citing sources and linking to other authorities is a good technique, but it is also good SEO — those outbound links demonstrate to search engines that you know your stuff, and that you're associating with the right crowd.

### High-quality content:

- Is free of spelling and grammatical errors. Proofread. And then have someone else proofread. (No joke, my mother sent me a screenshot of a grammatical error in a top company's Facebook post recently. Those are the people you need in your life.)
- links to good, reputable sources. Wikipedia counts as a good source to Google, no matter what your high school social studies teacher said.
- Has been fact-checked. Just because everyone else quotes that statistic, it does not mean you should, unless you can find the source.

## Check your keyword usage

You started with keywords and user intent research, of course, so this is not about figuring out which keywords apply to the piece of content in question. This is about examining how that keyword is being used in said content.

It is true that keyword stuffing, or linking content to every keyword it remotely relates to, is very, very out. It was never cool in the first place, but now — thanks to Google — it is also ineffective if not dangerous. It is also true that Google is very savvy about keywords. None of that, however, means that keywords are "dead." It just means SEO needs to use them better.

It is also worth noting that users look for keywords. Google is smart enough to recognize common synonyms, but when a user types in a keyword, he/she is looking for that bolded keyword.

## High-quality content:

- Is not stuffed full of the primary keyword. There is no real math for this. A good way to visualize is to use the "Find" feature in your document and search the keyword. If it looks oversaturated, start plugging in some synonyms.
- Organizes thematic subsections by primary related keywords. Google is getting better and better at understanding related terms. Do not be afraid of it.
- Makes natural use of keywords and variants in content. Do not overthink it. Use synonyms, abbreviations, plurals and so on like a normal human being.
- Makes natural use of keywords in image text. Image titles, alt text, and captions are strategic places for descriptive language. Do not force keywords but do use them as applicable.
- Makes natural use of keywords in titles. Write for people first, but if you can keep that target keyword toward the front of your title and/or first heading, do so.
- Makes natural use of keywords in the URL. This should not be too hard if you've used it in the title.
- Makes natural use of keywords and variants in the first 100 words. Do not be awkward, but do, as much as possible, lay all your cards on the table as quickly as possible

## Additional Information

I have heavily borrowed from the internet for this content, where else to get the details of what to do on the internet. You can read more about SEO at the following sites:

- https://www.searchenginejournal.com/seo-guide/
- https://searchengineland.com/complete-guide-optimizing-content-seo-checklist-269884
- https://moz.com/beginners-guide-to-seo
- https://blog.bufferapp.com/beginners-guide-to-seo

All this will help you deliver some good talking points to the target audience. As a growing business, it is critical to stay engaged with the customer and this is what will keep the business relevant in the minds of the customer over a period.

# 11 MARKETING YOURSELF AND YOUR IDEA

Making your message known – building a positive brand image

Your e-commerce business is up and running, you are established, and now you need to let the rest of the world know about all of the great things that you have to offer. It is time to focus on marketing your business: attracting new customers while keeping your current ones engaged and satisfied. To build a loyal customer base—and a great brand—you need an e-commerce marketing strategy.

E-commerce marketing may seem daunting at first, but it is actually rewarding and can be a lot of fun. We start with highlighting the most important of fundamentals here and we have some recommendations and best practices.

Figure 50: There are many different types of marketing platforms

## Make interactions more meaningful with personalization.

Personalized content is a powerful tool for rising above the marketing noise that pervades customers' online experience. Personalization can come in the form of emails containing links to related blogs, newsletters, and online videos. It can even be a simple (but loyalty-building) birthday email with special offers. Additionally, using you client's names in an email is good in a very limited sense, just do not add too much detail that creep people out. For personalized website content, there are many plugins and platforms that make custom tailoring of site content – based on customers' preferences and interactions – easier and more affordable than ever.

## Develop an Opt-in Email List

The other day, I was talking with one of my colleagues, and he asked me why anyone would want to build an email list. He gets all kinds of spam email and has learned to hate the companies that barrage your inbox with unwanted offers as a result. In fact, I suspect he subscribed to these various lists one way or another and just did not realize it at the time. Nevertheless, he makes a good point and it is always good to begin the process by understanding the underlying motivations.

The most powerful tool in online "email" marketing is to build an opt-in mailing list. An opt-in mailing list is a database of peoples' names and email addresses that have subscribed to an email list via a web form giving that list owner permission to send them periodic emails on the topic they are interested in. The best gift of this powerful tool is the possibility of being able to talk to people who are particularly interested in your product, service, or organization.

There are many reasons to develop an opt-in email list, but this section will focus on just three.

The internet is a fascinating place. People can visit your site from any corner of the globe and in most cases, you may never know they were there. Yes, there are traffic monitors and analytics platforms that can give you a lot of information about your website's visitors, but the fact remains that you never SAW the visitor, you never shook hands, you never said hello. This lies in stark contrast to the corner stores of yesteryear. Building an email list is an effective way to quantify your audience and know who you are speaking to. So quantifying your audience is the first reason.

The second reason is to build a massive email list is to have a way of contacting these people in the future when you've expanded your products or service offering. These are people who found you all on their own. They are watching you, whether you like it or not. And if you have a new product you are introducing, they will have some natural interest in hearing about it since they have already demonstrated a pervious interest in your product or service. More importantly, you can contact these people and sell them products with absolutely zero marketing expense because they have given you the information and pseudo-permission to install it.

The third reason to accumulate email addresses is that it contributes real value to your business. In other words, if you sold your business one day and you had a large opt-in email list of customers, you would get more money for your business because of these 'leads' and people who have demonstrated interest in the product that could be a source of potential info. Everybody knows these email lists represent a way of selling products with zero marketing expense and that means the company's profitability benefits by having the list. If you want to maximize the value of your business, you are well advised to start building an email list today.

As a business owner, there's always something else you have to do. It seems like your job is never over. And the task of building an email list is just one more thing you have to think about. But believe me; this task can contribute far more to your business than most others. The best approach is to integrate the task into your regular business. Find a way of accumulating email addresses without having to create a separate process.

Giveaway items are a great way to generate email lists. By offering something simple that would provide value to a potential customer, you will be able to capture their emails and then market directly to them.

Another way to get emails is to provide a helpful email in return of someone providing their email address. Some people like to get an email that would potentially detail a guide on how they can use your product or service to make their lives better.

After a while, you will end up with a real asset on your hands – one that can be tapped or sold at any time. Nothing wrong with that!

This gaining popularity of building opt-in mailing list is known as Permission Email Marketing.

There are do's and don'ts in starting your opt-in mailing list. Here are some of the most important tips worth mentioning:

DO
1. Put a subscription form prominently on your website. You can create your own subscription form using a software or by hiring a web developer to create this system for you.
2. Inform people that they can subscribe to your email list on the signature of your normal work emails. By using your work email account, every email you send will have the link to sign up for the mailing list in the footer. This will not only build credibility between you and your clients, but also allow anyone to easily sign up for the mailing list. Having the link to sign up for the mailing list in the footer of your work emails will be beneficial because everyone you email will also see it.
3. Ask people permission if they do want to be subscribed on your mailing list. This will prevent your customers from thinking that they are receiving unnecessary spam email.
4. Be clear on how people can benefit from subscribing and how often will you contact them. Make them know exactly what they will be receiving. This helps build credibility as well was lets your customers know that you respect their time and email inbox.
5. If you can, contact new subscriber as soon as you can. Welcome them with notes and tell them what to expect. In many cases, this process could be automated through the email marketing system that is used.

DON'T

1. Do not purchase lists that you are not 100% sure that are opt-in. Always have evidence to prove the legitimacy of the opt-ins. Sending email is pointless if it is not targeted and wanted. People would just automatically delete it or leave it unread if it seems unwanted.

2. Do not add everyone who has ever emailed you to your list. Always ask permission first or have them sign up through your website.

3. Do not abuse people's trust. This is a sure way to ruin you and your brand. Soon enough they will ignore your messages.

Building your opt-in mailing list is cheaper than in sending direct mails. Printing, envelopes, and paper used as material further add up to the cost. Here are some ways to effectively start your opt-in mailing list:

1. Offer a Free Newsletter. One of the most effective ways to build an opt-in list is to offer your online visitors freebies of value such as newsletter which will contain information that they can relate to such as tips, tools, recipes, travel itineraries and others. In some cases, companies will even do a quick industry news roundup for their email lists on topic that they would be interested in.

2. Make it Easy to Subscribe. Provide easy steps for subscription so that subscribers may find it easy to do so and would not be discouraged from signing up. For more subscribers, tell them the exact benefits they can get out of the subscription and the frequency of the mail they will receive on the page when the user signs up for the list.

3. Offer Quality Content. Be sure that what is written inside the newsletter, freebies, and information found in your website are all of value to increase visitors dropping by your website.

4. Participate in Forums. Discussion boards and forums are all

over the net. Try to actively participate in these boards especially those in the line of your interest or your business. I have mentioned this in many other places in this book, because it is incredibly important to participate not only during the formation of your business and gaining those initial customers, but continually in a way that allows you to network and grow with others in the industry. Try to build your reputation with credibility. In your forum discussions, always use signature ads where you can write a little about your services or product in the footer of your forum posts. Something simple could be linking to your website.

5.  Write articles and post them. This makes you an instant expert in your chosen field of interest because you are smart enough to write about it and share your insight. Make sure that you write articles that are relevant to your business goals and illustrate your expertise in the industry you have chosen.

6.  Write an eBook. An eBook is an excellent freebie for those who visited and subscribe in your mailing list. The eBook does not have to be expensively made or elaborate but it can be a compilation or a collection of best articles, business tips and resources.

In order to continue the growth of your email list, some good things to keep in mind are as follows:

## Spread the Word

Get others to sign up for your mailing lists with their consent. Spread the word about your mailing list through word of mouth. The beauty in this is that the list of emails will be self-screened, and the database will only contain the people who are interested in your offers. Make sure you have their consent beforehand. You do not want to risk losing reputation or SPAM penalties.

# Persistence

Before the internet, they used to say it takes around 7.3 impressions to make an impact with an ad. Today I would guess it to be over twice as high with the internet present. Make sure you are reaching out to your clients at least once a month in emails or other medium. Just because you emailed a list of people and had little or no response does not necessarily mean your audience is not interested in your product. Experiment with different emails, get to know which email strategy works best, and keep using it to reach out to your audience.

## Your Customers Want Useful Information

Emails should contain something that the customer wants. It should not be just a summary of your company or your resume. Focus on giving more than just what you sell. Specific content, messages, and other targeted information that interests your customers are good to include. For example, if you were selling makeup, you may want to include advice on how to apply the makeup or any makeup in general.

## Make Sure Your Audience Reads Your Emails

Graphics, animations, and logos are often blocked by email browsers, especially in the business market. Although they look impressive on an email, they will often lower your impression statistics if the pages do not render properly on the client's side. I recommend using flat text with hyperlinks to your site as well as styling the html elements in the email to look nice without any external images in case the email client will be unable to view those images. That way, the email looks good in both formats. Once your users get to your site, you can show them as many graphics as you want.

Cold call email marketing is becoming less and less effective in both return on investment as well as recipient conversion.

It is easy to see why some might think that mass coverage email marketing is a good idea. The premise is the more people who receive the email, the more likely client conversions there will be.

While this approach may be touted as one of the best ways to tap into a potentially huge market I'd like to explain why this approach rarely works.

1.  Cold calls do not work. Reports continue to surface that indicate whether it is face-to-face or online cold call marketing is highly ineffective. Therefore, there are fewer and fewer door-to-door salesmen. Gone are the days when a vacuum cleaner salesman would show up at your door and practically insist on showing you how the vacuum works and why it will save you time and money. I think it is very likely that telemarketing, and people's very strong dislike for that has made cold call marketing extremely difficult.

2.  Cold call marketing is rarely targeted. Most email lists that can be purchased or rented are not developed to pass along specific details on the buying habits or personal interests of the email addresses listed. There may be a few, but most of the time they are simply addresses that have been gleaned from a variety of sources and are simply sold to those most willing to pay. They may have not even chosen to receive emails from that specific industry in the first place.

3.  Spam filters hate cold call marketing. If you are sending material that was not requested by the recipient, it is likely most spam filters will catch and detain the majority of cold call email marketing attempts. Because of undesired marketing emails, spam filters have adjusted to take note of what types of emails should never be allowed to reach the recipient's inbox. Sometimes an email will slip through, but most of the time they will not.

## Raise your profile with search engine marketing (SEM).

Another way to stand out from the crowd is through search engine marketing (SEM). SEM is a type of paid advertising that promotes your website based on search terms (aka keywords) that you choose beforehand. SEM can raise the visibility of your e-commerce business on search engine results pages, making customers more likely to encounter your brand as they search for specific products or services.

## Get strategic with email marketing.

Email marketing is still one of the most effective ways to promote your business and sell your products and services to both existing and prospective customers. Proper email marketing is both an art and a science. There are dozens of best practices for a successful program, especially with regard to delivery and spamming. Therefore, perhaps the most important is to consider partnering with a third-party email delivery service. It is less work for you, and you don't need to worry about being categorized as a spammer. And their easy-to-use HTML templates mean you will not risk looking like an amateur. Most services also offer data tracking and reporting.

*Figure 51: In today's world, social media drives sales!*

## Use social media to drive sales.

Building relationships with customers through social channels such as Facebook and Twitter can help you grow your brand and generate sales – especially since existing customers' referrals are your best tool for getting new customers. If you decide to use social platforms as part of your marketing strategy, be prepared for significant hands-on effort. You will need to update your social media regularly to keep it fresh and to keep engaging with your customers. However, it is a great way to build your relationships with our customers, strengthen your brand and establish yourself as a thought leader. It is also important to note that social media is a two-way street: if a customer reaches out to you, you must respond promptly—otherwise, you risk damaging your business's reputation.

## Maintain a blog with valuable, quality information

While blogging is important for all types of businesses, it is particularly important for online businesses. Regularly writing blog posts that provide relevant information to your target market not only helps to establish trust and authority with your audience, it drives much-needed traffic to your site.

In fact, according to HubSpot's Marketing Benchmarks report, companies that blog 15 or more times each month receive 5 times more traffic than companies that do not blog. And this traffic ultimately translates into important leads: companies that increase their blogging from 3-5x per month to just 6-8 per month almost double their leads. That is a significant increase in leads for just a few extra blogs posts each month.

One of the main challenges that business owners have when it comes to blogging is knowing what to write about. They assume they need to write about their products or business and wonder how much they can really write on these topics. This is exactly the wrong strategy! Instead, focus on providing solutions to your target market's problems. What are the challenges and issues they face? What do they need help with? How can you help them with these problems? As you continue to provide relevant and valuable information, you will become a trusted source of information. And when your audience comes to trust you, they will be more likely to buy from you.

Make sure your website and content are properly optimized for SEO You do not have to be an SEO expert to understand and implement the fundamentals of SEO as I have mentioned earlier. One of the most important ways to get your site ranking in the search engines is to make sure you are using the keywords your target market will be looking for. Once you have decided which keywords to target, you'll want to make sure you use these (where appropriate and relevant) throughout your site, in your:

- URLs
- Title tags

- Heading tags (H1, H2, etc.)
- Alt image tags
- Content

Another factor that is important for SEO is regularly adding new blog posts and focusing on long form (1000 word+), 'meaty' content that covers every angle of a topic. Posts that do a great job of being a complete resource on a topic are likely to be popular with your audience and to receive inbound links from other sites. And getting inbound links is great both for SEO and for driving referral traffic back to your site.

## Become a guest on popular sites in your industry

When you blog on your own site, you connect with your current audience. But when you guest blog, you have the opportunity to reach a new audience who otherwise may never have found out about you.

There are other distinct advantages to guest blogging:

- Driving referral traffic to your site
- Aligning your brand with industry leaders
- Building your personal brand
- Establishing yourself as a thought leader in your field
- Generating new leads

A strategy often recommended before one jumps into guest blogging is making sure you have at least 10 amazing pieces of content on your site. This way, when you contact big-name publishers to ask about guest blogging opportunities, they can see what you are capable of providing. Some publishers will also allow you to link to your own content within your guest posts, so having these 10 articles will also give you something valuable to link to and drive more visits to your site.

There are other ways to leverage major brands other than guest blogging, too.

By understanding and implementing these strategies above, you will be head and shoulders above most online business owners. Recognizing that offering true value to your audience via blog posts, email, and social media content will help you reach and connect with your prospects and generate new leads.

## Making a Good Advertisement

Many small businesses do not get success they want from advertising due to availability of very little resources. The results are simply flat due to lack of good ideas for improvements. Whether the ads are put in a local newspaper or are plastered everywhere on the web, the money invested should gain the desired outcome. There are some common mistakes small businesses and professional service providers do when designing and posting the advertisement, which leads to the failure of the advertisement.

'Bigger is better' is a phrase believed in by many. That is exactly what some of the small firms think when they want to advertise their product. They think bigger and select a medium where they need to invest a lot of money, but do not reach the targeted market. Like if a company specializes in designing diet plans and want to help out people who had disappointing results from their individual diet plans, and the company chooses to advertise a full page in the local paper instead of running advertisement in a health magazine, obviously not many of the dieters will notice the advertisement and the advertisement doesn't get the desired attention.

The point is to come up with the best campaign, which will increase the probability of the ad getting viewed and the right customers trying to buy the product or sign up for the service. Studies and research can be carried out on the market and targeted audience can be narrowed down. Once you have made a list of places where your customers look for information meant for the customers in mind, find out how many readers they have and the cost they ask for posting the ad. Special deals are offered by different ad networks from time to time and can only be found by watchful eye.

It is estimated that everyday people are subjected to around three thousand commercials. That is a huge number and if someone desires to be noticed, their ad should certainly be different from the rest. Not only the services and product sold should be unique in the market, so should be the advertisement. For example, if a business selling mattresses says, "We sell mattresses", it will not make a statement and will be passed off as any other mattress advertisement. But if they say, "Our mattresses are of the finest quality", it will make the advertisement stand out in the crowd. Other catch lines are "Are you suffering from back pain? You must try our mattresses!", are more specific and will catch the fancy of the people who are suffering from chronic back pains. The advertisement should also focus on the uniqueness of the product and how it is better compared to the competitors' product.

Focusing on the problems of the customers and giving a solution for them, is what a customer demands. A customer does not buy a product; he buys benefits in the form of a product. The real value of the product should be realized and a clear picture of it should be presented to the customer so he will be able to relate with the product. If the advertisement does not specify the solution it can provide, the customers will never know of it. Focusing on the customers problem is what some ads miss.

The last thing missing in most of the advertisement is motivation for the customers. If the advertiser has designed the advertisement and the customer had read the advertisement, all efforts and money invested will be wasted if he does not get up and do something about it. It should not be assumed that the customer knows what to do; instead the advertisement should influence the mind of the customer and should tell them what to do. Call of action is the final job of the advertisement. It should call for information or visiting the store or even visiting the online store. The message should sound confident and clear.

## Some Free Forms of Advertisement

You have finished building your own website. You have introduced your company and presented your products and services. You have added propositions and promos to catch your target audience's attention.

Free promotions such as search engines and directories would give your web site the deserved traffic you always wanted. Make sure to check your web site's ranking to know whether or not this type of free promotion is right for you.

Make a deal with other web sites on trading links which could help both web sites. Make sure to use words that could easily interest the audience.

Find free classified ads web sites that could boost the promotion of your web site. Most of these classified ads web sites provide powerful marketing features and are an extremely fast way of getting your products or services online.

Free and low-cost internet banners are spread all throughout the Internet. Banners that pop-up at the top of a page or in a separate window would automatically catch your target audience's attention but would be considered devious and annoying in today's world.

Free internet advertising is a perfect way to make your products or services known to millions of prospective Internet customers. The probability of someone needing your services or wanting to buy your products is very high. There are free advertising opportunities out there that may suit your services, products, and web site…you just need to find them! Go to work – Browse the internet for the best free internet advertising and learn how to take advantage of what you are able to find.

If at first you do not succeed…try, try again! Analyze your techniques, keep track of your customers, and learn what works. Then be ready to try new methods and repeat those methods that are already working.

It has been said that the best things in life are free and this saying also applies to the many forms of free advertising that are available on the internet, you just need to talk to people and find them!

## Pay Per Click Advertising

Offline advertising is growing by 7% per year, while internet advertising is speeding ahead with a 32% annual growth rate. Traditional media is losing its market share as companies increasingly move their ads to the online media, specifically in the paid search arena.

Advertising in online media has some definite advantages over offline media in terms of cost, reach, interactivity, targeting the right markets and measuring responses. This is why internet advertising is now becoming hot property for marketers!

Of all advertising (telemarketing, magazine advertising, newspapers, radio, TV, banner ads, email marketing, etc.), PPC advertising provides the most qualified leads and is proven to have the highest sales conversion rate. This is because, unlike other forms of advertising, your ad is only displayed when your prospective customer is searching for your products or services. This is why nearly 40% of all online advertisements are now pay per click campaigns.

The trend of advertisements within the online medium is fast changing too. While search engine optimization is becoming vital for making your website emerge above competition, pay per click advertising is providing a very cost-effective means to reach your target audience.

According to The Kelsey Group and ConStat, Inc, small-business PPC advertisers currently allocate on average 23% of their total advertising budget to PPC activities. Of these, 54% expect to increase their PPC spending the next year. Paid search has undoubtedly become the hottest means of online advertising.

## What is a PPC Ad?

Pay per click campaigns (PPC) are defined as the guaranteed placement of a small "ads" on the search results page for a specific keyword or keywords. Your PPC ads are displayed when a user searches for your services or products. This means PPC ads are targeting those customers who are actively seeking your product or services and therefore are already looking to spend money.

No matter what your budget is, you only need to pay for the customers who click your link. PPC campaigns are suitable for all types of businesses.

## Major PPC campaigns

There are two major pay per click campaigns: Google AdWords, owned by Google and Yahoo! Search Marketing, which is Yahoo's PPC service.

Pay per click advertising is growing at a very fast pace but has recently become extremely competitive. As a result, PPC campaigns need to be professionally managed to ensure the best return on investment.

## Advantages of PPC Advertising

**Speed**: PPC reaches its target market at a fast rate as compared to other online and offline advertisements. You can have an ad up and running in less than an hour.

**Sales Lead**: Pay Per Click advertising generates more qualified leads as compared to other advertising media, as it targets customers who are actively seeking out your products or services.

**Track the lead conversion**: You can track the lead conversion of a PPC campaign very easily. You can see exactly how people find your ad and appeal to their exact questions and concerns through the dashboard of the campaign manager.

**Cost**: PPC is a cost-effective means of reaching global customers, much cheaper than traditional media, which is usually limited to the immediate audience within its reach, be it TV, radio, or print. Only web marketing can give you global reach at such a cost-effective rate. Unfortunately, in recent years this difference in the price is becoming less apparent as the market becomes more crowded and more searches are used.

**Ongoing improvements**: In a newspaper ad, if it contains bad ad copy, it is likely that no one will respond, and all your money goes down the drain. The costs would include paying the ad agency for the ad and then the newspaper/publication for the ad space. Similarly, in the case of radio or television, if your ad campaign is not appealing or convincing, the whole effort and money investment is simply going to go waste. If no one clicks your PPC ad, you will not lose money as you would not have incurred much of a cost, and you can tweak the ad copy, until you achieve results you want.

## Word of Mouth – Your Best form of Advertising

Even though we are building a business based on the internet, word of mouth advertising is incredibly powerful for generating leads in your local community. Word of mouth advertising creates an awareness campaign where your business information travels from person to person. For a new business start-up, word of mouth marketing is often the best and most effective advertising method.

Newspaper print and classified ads can get very expensive and have lost much of their effectiveness with the popularity of the internet. New business owners cannot even consider radio or television advertising as a viable option due to the outstanding costs.

Here are some steps that you can take to start a viral word of mouth marketing campaign about your business:

Acquaintances: Approach your friends, family, and neighbors initially, followed by contacting other people you know in your community and beyond. To begin your campaign, you may take a broad approach to spread your information; ultimately streamlining your message to your target market.

Networking: Both online and off, networking is the backbone of the word of mouth marketing. You need to have a large network to build a database of prospective customers. Find forums and other groups where your target market 'hang out.'

Establish your website with good, focused keywords to get favorable results from the search engines. Also, keep your website, user-friendly with easy navigation and complete updated information about everything regarding your business.

Freebies: Everyone loves to get something free. Create a free report or eBook related to your idea or product and give it away to potential customers, asking them to give the item to their friends and family as well.

Word of mouth advertising has stood the test of time and is effective for every business.

In our 3D printer business, it would help to create PPC adds on social media accounts of people who would be needing to buy gifts for people or who enjoy custom experiences. Luckily due to the nature of the social media accounts we use, we can target these ads directly to the people we want to sell to. In addition, we will be creating a blog on the company website as well as a mailing list with curated featured projects, products, and blog articles about the industry in general. This will allow us to be able to keep out current customers interested as well as keep them shopping. Finally, in order to make customers retained further, we will be offering them coupon codes for their birthday so they can purchase a custom 3d printed object for themselves as their own gift. By taking these steps, we will be able to reach new clients and keep current ones happy.

## Additional Information

Given that marketing online is in itself a complete field of study, you will get a lot of inputs and will have to spend considerable time doing this. You can engage an online marketing agency for ensuring that the basics are in place. Engaging with a good content writer is also advisable if you have limited time to put a blog together. Multiple online resources will tell you the ways of marketing an online business. The more you explore the more there is to learn in this field. Try the following for starters:

- https://www.americanexpress.com/us/small-business/openforum/articles/7-ways-to-promote-your-business-online-for-free/
- https://www.entrepreneur.com/article/283832
- https://searchenginewatch.com/sew/how-to/2048588/30-free-ways-to-market-your-small-business-site
- https://www.thebalance.com/how-to-market-your-business-online-for-free-4042529
- https://marketingland.com/21-ways-market-business-online-shoestring-budget-127277
- https://www.wix.com/blog/2016/12/free-places-to-promote-your-website/
- https://www.smartinsights.com/marketplace-analysis/customer-analysis/10-free-online-marketing-tools-that-every-hands-on-marketer-should-use/
- https://www.entrepreneur.com/article/288385
- https://www.inc.com/jayson-demers/your-guide-to-marketing-an-online-business.html
- http://www.twelveskip.com/marketing/strategies/1425/market-your-business-online
- https://www.allbusiness.com/slideshow/ten-key-steps-to-successfully-marketing-your-business-online-16672669-1.html

# 12 GROWTH—THE DETAILS

Continuous innovation can keep you ahead

The true success of a business is in its ability to grow over the years. If we have done the groundwork well and we keep listening to our customers, then we will continually be able to grow not just in our own location, but we will be able to expand into new markets as well.

Growth comes with higher sales. When you spend most of your time selling, opportunities quickly arise. Doors open. Checks get written. Good things happen. When you stay in your office talking to your staff, pontificating over product details, stuck in a rut of admin and minutiae you may progress your business, but you will not greatly increase your revenue.

Only going out there and asking more people to buy your new and interesting stuff will make a real difference in the long run. All else is tinkering at the peripheries of success. How much time should you spend on sales? Well if you are running a new business you should devote at least 80 % of your day to it. If you are an established business, you should spend at least 30% of your day on the sales process or connecting with customers.

Sales should be the absolute center of what your company does, every single day. Ignore it at your peril. As the founder of IBM, Thomas Watson once remarked, "Nothing happens until somebody sells something." And do not allow any resistance from your sales staff about being pushed and held accountable either. All salespeople must be ready for their performance being closely monitored. Sales are too important not to have a constant magnifying glass on it. In terms of a single man operation, you still must take sales into account while trying to balance everything. Easier said than done, but you should be pursuing sales leads as they appear so you have a constant flow of work to keep you busy.

*Figure 52: Watch your investment grow!*

# Growth Momentum Areas

There are many areas that if approached well will result in building the growth momentum, we highlight a few examples here:

## Bill faster

Your receivables can count for 40 – 50% of your actual assets. Do not batch invoice: bill as soon as you can. Even if it leads to multiple smaller orders just book sales faster.

## Simplify your business

Weed out the unprofitable and the hard-to-sell. Make your product portfolio as targeted to your audience as possible

## Simplify your marketing message

Let your audience connect with the business, make it simple to understand and the message should always try to lead people to information that helps them buy. This includes details of website and buying options.

## Get your business and your website listed in relevant directories

The more places that have a reference to your business the easier it is for a potential customer to locate you. No one can be present at every possible touch point; this also means that even if you think you have covered every touchpoint there is one more to link to. To find directories, Google the name of your town plus directories URL".

## Learn to delegate

Figure out what you do that turns dollars. Then delegate the rest. Focus on sales much more than anything else. Sales will keep you in direct touch with customers which is where all the learning for growth is. Listen to the customer as much as you can.

## Encourage employees to Innovate

It is helpful to encourage employees to find new ways to their tasks that makes it easier on them instead of relying on their standard way of doing things. Push for process innovation, look for small changes that can reduce time to delivery or can enhance customer experience. Run a small content within the organization that rewards process innovators.

## Do not forget suppliers

They might not be on your payroll, but they are more apt to do a few things for you at no charge because you really take care of them. Ensure timely payments and a healthy contact between you and the suppliers, innovative ideas about product or supply chain can well come from the field knowledge that your suppliers have.

## Work faster

If you can condense three four-month jobs into three three-month jobs, you can do one more job in the year. This links back to the process innovation story, everything that speeds up delivery to the customer will help you do more in the market and probably take up more jobs helping growth.

## Reward your team for meeting budgets and timelines

A 5% bonus is cheaper than a 20% increase in costs. Also, this helps build a winning culture, give longevity to your employees, and brings stability to the organization.

## Cut overhead by automating most of the non-producing items

Automation is your friend in a non-customer experience impacting way! Some tasks like accounting, remedial customer care, voice mail, sales reporting, ordering, and record keeping can be easily automated. Shift as much routine work to automation as you possibly can, this is mostly cost and not directly adding new customers to the business.

## Make sure you have clearly outlined project scope

When assigning tasks and projects, make it clear what the objectives are and do not be afraid to charge your customer for changes.

## Offer to be a spokesperson for your specialty

When your local media outlets need an expert opinion, volunteer to help and give your perspective... It is free marketing and builds credibility! Send them a relevant press release every month.

## Give something valuable away on your website

Give something of decent value to a potential customer away free of charge on your website; at your front counter; when you send out your invoices, or when you deliver goods. This should be free to you, but valuable to the recipient, for example, coupons or a "How To" guide.

## Highlight offers, features, promotions, and news

Highlight offers, features, promotions, and news in your email footers, invoices, and letter signatures. All marketing communication should talk about the running offers and your product/service differentiators.

## Go where your audience is on the web.

If your potential audience hangs out on forums, then post to those forums. Become a trusted advisor.

## Get your supporters to refer you.

Check out "Make A Referral Week" to learn more about how referrals can build a business.

# Getting Referrals

Referrals are the key to exponential and cost-efficient business growth.

In order to have your current customer refer you another, supply a top-notch product. Let your customers know how advantageous your brand is and provide exceptional service. Do that and you will encourage customers to willingly send their families, friends, acquaintances, and business associates your way.

There is no easier sale than the sale made to a "pre-sold" prospect. This kind of favorable condition can only arise as a result of the shared enthusiasm from another delighted buyer. Word-of-mouth advertising generates top quality referrals. As a marketing tool, it simply cannot be beat. Word of mouth promotion cannot be purchased for any amount of money... it can only be earned.

Referrals happen when one friend willingly shares information with another. What makes referrals so effective is that no true friend would recommend a business, service, or product that they did not completely approve of themselves.

The foundation for building your business with referrals is a solid product or service -- one that not only meets but exceeds your advertising claims. One way to achieve customer satisfaction is to "under promise" and "over deliver".

This does not mean you should weaken your advertising materials. Simply focus on providing more for you customers – more than you promise. That is another formula for success. People are always thrilled to get a little something extra with a purchase they are already happy about.

Write powerful sales copy that clearly positions your product as the overwhelming favorite. Make a huge promise... and deliver even more.

Treat your customers as the most important component of your business. Customers are vital to your success – even to your very existence. People want to be treated fairly, with respect, and courtesy. The golden rule still applies – treat people the same way you like to be treated. Remember, nobody likes to wait beyond a reasonable amount of time for an order to be filled.

When you get in the habit of delighting customers, you will find that people are overly happy and tell others. As word spreads about your product or service, your business is propelled to new heights.

Your success in business is predicated on your ability to satisfy customers, and to continuously grow your customer base. In all your communications with customers, you need to encourage them tell others about all the benefits your product or service offers.

Let loyal buyers know that you are always seeking new customers. Remind newsletter readers that you have built your business by thoroughly satisfying customers and having those customers tell others in turn.

Ask buyers if they know anyone who would like and could benefit from your catalogue. As soon as a name is provided, fire off an introduction email... and send a thank you note to the customer who fed you the lead. Referrals make it easy to grow your business.

If you really want to make people stick around after you find a new lead, provide discount cards for new customers. Offer a 10% to 15% discount on their first purchase and then make these available to your existing customers for distribution to others. Give them an extra reason for handing these discount coupons out.

Offer points towards free gifts, free premiums, for each discount coupon redeemed, or simply acknowledge them as a "builder" of your organization, complete with their picture and certificate, proudly displayed for all to see.

The best way to get customers to refer others is "in the moment" -- when they're still enamored with your product or your high level of personal service right after you deliver your project or get off a great support call with someone.

While customers are enjoying these positive emotions about your company, that is the time to ask for a little favor. Ask "Is there someone else you know, who might want to grow their business by 37%this year? or get that older car looking showroom-clean? Or transform any weed-filled lot into a lush green lawn and garden?

Simply fill in the end of the sentence with the big benefit you have just delivered on. Plant the seed of referrals and referrals will come your way.

## Rules of Growth

For years, I have tried to answer this one question: What do small businesses that achieve sustained growth do differently from those that do not grow? There are, seven specific areas in which growth companies concentrate their efforts.

1.  Strong sense of purpose. Most leaders of companies that have achieved growth discover that it takes more than the promise of increasing financial reward to fuel their aspirations and ambitions. They find a higher calling than simply the pursuit of "more money."
2.  Outstanding market intelligence. This is an organization's ability to first recognize, then adapt, to fundamental changes in the marketplace. Many times, small-business owners become too myopic, seeing only a limited view of the markets in which they compete. Growth leaders see the bigger picture.
3.  Effective growth planning. This is the best predictor of whether or not a business will grow. To be effective, a plan

for growth does not need to be overly formal or complicated. However, it does need to be written, well-communicated and regularly updated.

4.  Customer-driven processes. These days, every company I talk to believes it is customer-driven, when actually very few really are. Take a look at all of the business processes from a customer's perspective. Are they in place to make it easier for the company, or to help deliver on the promise of faster, cheaper, and better for the customer?

5.  The power of technology. Successful leaders do not let the boom and bust of technology cycles give them the excuse to ignore that we live in an information age. If a company is in business, it is in the technology business.

6.  The best and brightest people. Growth leaders recognize that they are only as good as the people with whom they work. The ability to hire, train and retain the best and the brightest people is often the difference between success and failure.

7.  Seeing the future. Few organizations take the time to regularly consider the future. Growth leaders learn how to diligently monitor and interpret the macro forces of change affecting the world in which they live.

By adapting these rules of growth and combining some of the strategies above, you will be able to grow your business.

My professors always told me that the key to success is outgrowing and outpacing the compeition, and I believe that by adopting some of these strategies, you will be able to outgrow competition.

*Figure 53: Different factors lead to different types of growth.*

## Growth Factors

Growth has a direct link with the kind of team you have, as the business grows it is important to hire a team and get the momentum going. Hiring is a difficult process, it requires you to find and trust people, it also requires you to delegate what you know you can do better and probably faster. The first question you must answer is – which team to hire first. Start we the front line as much as you can. Having more people to sell will help you get the growth momentum you are looking for but be advised the sales team requires the maximum amount of support from your end as well.

Invest in a good sales team, also get a good marketing person on your team. You do not need many people for marketing, but you do require a good person here. They will work as your extension in terms of listening to the market, the customers, the suppliers. They will be responsible to spread the word about the business and build a connect with the audience. They will maintain the relationship with the society and the media folks. They will maintain your social media accounts and help share information with the content writers for the blogs that help expand your reach. They will maintain consistency and freshness in your promotional campaigns and will keep a track of all these dollars going in the right direction. There is just so much that needs doing and this person will give that support to you.

Only after you have built a strong and performance-oriented sales and marketing team should you venture into expanding any other function in the organization. With expansion comes delegation, be flexible and patient the results will follow.

## Additional Information

Growing your business is a daily job, there is no stopping. One must be totally devoted to its promotion and spend as much energy trying to expand as much as we can. There is a host of ideas that help you focus on growth; it is a process and a mindset which will give you the direction in ensuring that the business grows in the long run. We have a few suggestions about resources that can help give you the required ideas.

- https://www.entrepreneur.com/slideshow/299772
- https://www.thebalance.com/top-ways-of-growing-your-business-2948140
- https://www.forbes.com/sites/siimonreynolds/2013/07/11/the-fastest-way-to-grow-your-business/
- https://articles.bplans.com/17-ideas-you-can-steal-to-grow-your-business-without-spending-money/

# 13 DIVERSIFYING YOUR PORTFOLIO
Time to start again!

In the last chapter, we spent some time discussing how to grow our business. The requirements of growth are such that we come to the discussion on diversification. Having a single business is a risk one should avoid. We are sure you have heard the old adage, "Don't put all your eggs in one basket." For a new business, this is extremely important, it is advice that should be taken quite seriously--especially in this digital age when product life cycles and customer sensibilities change overnight. A single line of business is at existential risk if a shift happens.

Many examples of international business can be seen where they vanished just because they were involved in only one line of business and the customer preferences changed rapidly. One such example can be of pager companies which could not become the next big mobile phone manufacturer and thus were wiped out by changing preferences. Mobile phone companies like Nokia have faced this issue with changing customer requirements. Similarly, the business models of traditional camera, film, and printing process companies like Kodak have also disappeared over time with the advent of digital photography and a fundamental shift in how people store a picture.

It is important to do everything we can to ensure that something like this does not happen to our small business. The most relevant answer is diversification, but it is an answer that is much more easily offered than implemented. You need to strap the thinking cap on tightly for this one and tap the most creative minds in your small business and the world outside. Actually, you have to start the complete thinking process again, the same process through which you started the original business in the first place. Here are some thoughts that will help kindle that fire in your mind.

*Figure 54: Think about small ways that you can change your product to apply it a different way.*

## Diversifying your product line-up

To start, adapt and tweak your product or service so it appeals to a new group of consumers or users. If you have a "high end" product or service, consider a less-expensive version. You need to be careful that you do not undercut yourself. In some cases, a "professional" and "hobbyist" version of the same product works well. This simply goes on to say that a different wallet size can be approached with simple changes to the product or service. Sometimes a better or different packaging and feature set can attract a differing set of customers. A Car company has various models to attract buyers from each segment. Similarly, an airline would have an economy, business, and first-class travel options. Even the clothes we buy would have different price ranges depending on the yarn used for the cloth.

## Find Related Products.

Can we find products that go along with what you sell or do that your customers or clients purchase from a different vendor? In Economics class, they teach you to call these dependent goods. Similar to how some coffee machines need specific pods to make coffee or coffee filters to brew the best coffee the machine can make. Perhaps there are training materials that you can offer as well. A medical equipment company, for example, found a new niche in providing ongoing training and support for its equipment. You can also establish a large business doing aftersales service or annual maintenance contracts for products you sell. This way the existing relationships can be leveraged, and revenue enhanced.

The most aggressive version of this strategy is to buy a company that makes products related to yours. If you can swing it, this can be a very smart move. You diversify your line-up and remove a potential competitor from the playing field. We have seen this a lot lately with companies such as Facebook and Amazon.

## Offer an integrated solution

This flows from the previous idea, and the basic question you need to ask yourself and your team is, "Can we do more?" This might be anything: training, cloud services, apps, additional gear, monitoring, servicing- the possibilities are endless.

Find out what is next. Are technological changes beginning to erode your client base? Do not be the last in your industry to sense where things are going. Devote part of your business to meeting the needs of the "early adopters," and then you will be ready if a major shift occurs.

*Figure 55: A cloud, not 'The Cloud'*

## Moving to the Cloud

There comes a point when every business has a decision to make in terms of their increasing infrastructural needs. At some point, you need to weigh the options of being onsite or offsite.

In today's world, the 'cloud' is all the buzz. The cloud is the offsite seemingly invisible amount of computing resources available for companies to use There are many big players in this industry and they have contracts with some of the biggest companies in the world. These large companies took their own data centers and decided that it would be more cost effective to close them down and move to another provider.

The cloud offers many additional forms of flexibility such as easy on demand scalable storage, compute, and bandwidth when you need it. In the scheme of cutting costs and scaling elegantly, there is no better way than with one of the big cloud providers.

It is not all great though, the costs of cloud could start to add up, especially if you account for growth that has not happened yet. Additionally, some of the services cloud providers offer may cost pennies by themselves, but are dependent on other systems, services, or products to work correctly and could cause high bills.

It is important to make sure you take into account the growth you expect in the future years, and how the expenses of moving to a cloud provider will impact at the time of the move.

## Open another location

If you are exclusively online, consider a physical location. If you have one physical location, consider opening a second. Look at markets that would be more open to your products that is if you have a large city presence then look at suburbs and the adjoining countryside. Leverage on the brand name you have created to sell to these communities.

*Figure 56: Expansion overseas is a growing trend today as businesses grow.*

## Go overseas

Not every small business has the wherewithal to launch an overseas operation. Right now, the big players are eyeing Africa the way they eyed Asia 10 years ago. Network in your community and see if any businesses are exploring overseas ventures. You might find a project where your company fits in. look for a master distributor for a region, a good partnership can give you a new market almost overnight.

## Follow the growth

If you are in an area with disheartening demographics or punishing tax rates, see if you should expand to a lower tax growth area. Would one of these areas be a good candidate for a branch office?

Smart business owners, like the smart investors, place a high value on diversification. Take time to draw up a good game plan for your company.

Building this plan is much like the way we started the work on the business in the first place. We must do a detailed gap analysis and then follow it up with market analysis and research. All this should be done to validate a hypothesis of expansion or new product launch. What is critical while you are doing all this is to ensure that no love is lost with the core business. We have to balance new products and expansion agenda while protecting the existing business.

# Keep on learning

As I have alluded to earlier, you need to be ripe for learning throughout your entire life and need not stay stagnant. As you also become more and more advanced in your specific field, it can help your company and credibility to receive some professional certifications, especially in the IT field.

IT Certifications are 'degrees' issued by a company or IT vendor that demonstrates your knowledge of working with their products and knowledge on how to properly manage, maintain, and architect robust solutions that would work well.

However, to really get ahead in today's market, you need a Microsoft certification, whether it is an MCP, MCSA, MCSE or any other string of letters. Quite a few people will go for multiple certifications to broaden their experience and scope of possible opportunities.

Some of the Microsoft certifications require you have to have at least one year of practical experience in order to pursue a certification, namely an MCSE or Microsoft Certified Systems Engineer. It is important to have that experience that these certain certifications require because the training, like the MCSE training and the MCSE exams that follow, are very intense. In fact, some people will not only partake of the standard MCSE training, but also MCSE boot camps and classes for more in-depth studies into their certification.

One standard benefit to having a Microsoft certification is that it is a great basic means of analyzing the aptitude of an employee. If you are a manager or owner in a business, you want some way to evaluate that employee's skills. And if you are the employee, you know that your boss recognizes your abilities.

If you do not have much hands-on experience in your field, but you do have the Microsoft certification to prove that you know the material, you would also have a leg up on anyone else applying to help the same clients. For some reason, that certification, those little string of letters like MCP or MCSE, hold a lot of power.

Yet another benefit to holding a Microsoft certification or two is the money aspect of it all. Sure, you shelled out some major bucks to fund your education in those MCP courses or that MCSE training, but consider it an investment in yourself. With certification, you can bargain more business and therefore a higher salary!

Many professionals could benefit from a Microsoft certification, as well as any other large vendor of IT resources. The more you know as a businessman and professional, the better position you can put your business in, the more money you stand to make.

So, think about going for your MCSE or MCP certification or any number of others available. More training; more knowledge; more money ... sounds like a no-brainer!

The Internet has an abundance of online resources of free and pay practice exam questions about information technology computer certification exams. There are many companies with high visibility websites that offer free practice exam and test questions to show that they are concerned about giving you some certification training. The practice exam questions that are more relevant to the actual certification exam will require a purchase but are well worth it. These websites are hoping that you will like the free practice test questions so you will want to purchase the detail ones that give you an explanation of the answer.

What are the advantages of purchasing computer certification practice test questions over the free practice exam questions that are available? Free practice exam questions can be helpful for those want to save on your learning expenses. Free practice exam questions are usually on the basics of information technology. The real in-depth material of any certification exam will have to be purchased. The best practice exam questions usually come at a moderate price.

Where does a student who is preparing for an IT certification exam find practice exam questions that are similar or practically identical to the real certification exam? Can there possibly be a place for a person to find practice test question on computer certification that would be just like the ones on the actual exam? What would you look for in finding the best and most applicable practice exam questions about the actual certification exam? I would look for a place that had up to date practice exam questions. Microsoft and others are constantly changing the test questions on the certification exams. All software companies have updates to their systems, so the test questions should change also.

If you had questions that were closer to the exam, wouldn't they be better prepared for the final certification exam? Knowing what is on the final certification exam can build your confidence and ability to pass it. I would say that there are very few places where you could find practice exam questions that would be the same as the actual certification exam and have the price be reasonable. This is on purpose, because exam providers would want to test your knowledge, not regurgitation skills.

Knowing what a certification test looks like and how to prepare for it would be very beneficial. Practice exam questions can tell you what material you should be studying for the final certification exam. No one can memorize all of the material related to an IT certification. Practice exam questions are very important to use in preparing for your certification exam.

Getting some advice from someone who has gone through the whole experience of receiving their certification would greatly help. Someone who has not only a success story to tell you about when passing a certification exam, but also can tell of a failure, or advice on what to look out for can allow you to be one step ahead. They probably could tell you where you could get the best computer training and find the best practice exam questions that would be the closest to the actual exam at a good price.

Most practice exams purchased will be quite numerous, 300 or more and there are only about 60 questions on the actual certification exam depending on the test. Is it possible to memorize all 300 questions to be completely prepared to take your certification exam? No, that is insane. Would it be more beneficial to actually learn the product and become better at reasoning through difficult questions? Yes. With time, dedication, and the right resources you can gain lifelong learning that allows you to position you and your business for success.

## Accounting principles

In positioning your business for success, keeping the right books are essential Accounting has been defined as, by Professor of Accounting at the University of Michigan William A Paton as having one basic function: "facilitating the administration of economic activity. This function has two closely related phases:

1. measuring and arraying economic data
2. communicating the results of this process to interested parties."

As an example, a company's accountants periodically measure the profit and loss for a month, a quarter or a fiscal year and publish these results in a statement of profit and loss that is called an income statement. These statements include elements such as accounts receivable (what is owed to the company) and accounts payable (what the company owes). It can also get pretty complicated with subjects like retained earnings and accelerated depreciation. All of this is quote overwhelming!

Much of accounting though, is also concerned with basic bookkeeping. This is the process that records every transaction; every bill paid, every dime owed, every dollar and cent spent and accumulated.

As a business owner, you are concerned with the summaries of these individual transactions, contained in the financial statement. The financial statement summarizes a company's assets. A value of an asset is what it cost when it was first acquired. The financial statement also records what the sources of the assets were. Some assets are in the form of loans that have to be paid back. Profits are also an asset of the business.

In what is called double-entry bookkeeping, the liabilities are also summarized. Obviously, a company wants to show a higher amount of assets to offset the liabilities and show a profit. The management of these two elements is the essence of accounting.

There is a system for doing this; not every company or individual can devise their own systems for accounting; the result would be chaos!

Anyone who is worked in an office at some point or another has had to go through accounting. They are the people who pay and send out the bills that keep the business running. They do a lot more than that, though. Sometimes referred to as "bean counters" they also keep their eye on profits, costs, and losses. Unless acting as your own accountant, you would have no way of knowing just how profitable - or not - your business is without some form of accounting.

No matter what business you are in, even if all you do is balance a checkbook, that's still accounting. It is part of even a kid's life. Saving an allowance, spending it all at once - these are accounting principles.

What are some other businesses where accounting is critical? Well, farmers need to follow careful accounting procedures. Many of them run their farms year to year by taking loans to plant the crops. If it is a good year, a profitable one, then they can pay off their loan; if not, they might have to carry the loan over, and accrue more interest charges.

Every business and every individual needs to have some kind of accounting system in their lives. Otherwise, the finances can get away from them, they do not know what they've spent, or whether they can expect a profit or a loss from their business. Staying on top of accounting, whether it's for a multi-billion-dollar business or for a personal checking account is a necessary activity on a daily basis if you're smart. Not doing so can mean anything from a bounced check or posting a loss to a company's shareholders. Both scenarios can be equally devastating.

Accounting is basically information, and this information is published periodically in business as a profit and loss statement, or an income statement.

In today's world most of the summary reports and calculations could be accomplished through a computerized accounting system. The major thing is just being sure you have the correct systems in place to allow for continued growth and platform diversification through proper accounting. I could write an entire book alone on this topic, but rest assured there are many wonderful online resources to access information on.

*Figure 57: Who Does accounting on pen and paper anymore?*

# Investing

Wise investments of your spare funds can be a great way to grow rich. These days, savings accounts offer very low interest and it is a waste to allow your money to lie in them. Based on your appetite for risk and your financial needs, you have various other investment schemes and options to choose from. I am not condoning investing all of your profits in other non-business ways, but it may be a good idea to invest in some other companies and reap the rewards of their successes as well to help the bottom line grow.

It is always safer to have a diversified portfolio, that is, to spread your money around in various types of schemes, so that the risks and returns get balanced out. For those of you with greater risk-taking ability, stock markets or mutual funds can be a good idea. In stock markets, you can buy shares of companies listed on the stock exchange.

As I have specified during the majority of the chapter, many businesses prefer to reinvest the profits into expansion projects instead of declaring dividends. These reinvestments in turn should lead to further profits. However, the stock markets are unpredictable and a lot of people who dabble in stocks with the purpose of making some quick bucks may end up with losses instead.

Mutual funds are relatively safer investments, though they are also subject to market risk. Mutual funds are investments made in the stock market by financial managers with a fund collected from actual investors. There can be sector-specific mutual funds for instance those that invest in Pharmaceutical or IT or infrastructure companies only. Whatever be the mode of your investment in the markets, it is vital that you track these on a regular basis. If the prices of your shares or mutual funds decline at a time when there is a slowdown in the economy as a whole, there is no need to panic and sell at a loss. The markets will quite likely bounce back to where they were or perhaps even better. However, if the markets are strong and yet, the value of your mutual funds is on a decline, it could mean it is not well invested and it would be advisable for you to sell and move your money into something that will generate better returns. A financial consultant can advise you about the market situation and what types of investments will suit your needs best.

# Franchising

If you have developed a business model that has worked for you, it may be a good idea to franchise that. Franchising is selling a business model to other people to repeat and taking a fee in royalties as they operate their business. Think of how fast food restaurants have many locations and all do the same thing. That business started out as one location and then found that their business model was repeatable and scalable, and they sold the concept, materials, and product to other people who believed they could make a profit doing the same thing.

# Licensing

Licensing is different from franchising in the respect that you are distributing copies of software or sharing the proprietary technology that you have developed with a third party for a set fee such that they can incorporate it into their product or service. In this way, you can retain the earnings from developing the software or product and the third party can

This is a similar way that people who own intellectual property make sure that they make money with their patents or copyrights. This is how you can see athletic team logos on pretty much everything and could be a great additional revenue stream.

How Can I diversify my business to increase sources of income?

_____

_____

_____

_____

_____

For our 3D printer business, we could one day potentially grow it into a platform in which people are able to custom order 3d printed parts and the system would be able to send it to a close location to be produced. This could act in a franchising model potentially. Using the extra funds of the business, we can make strategic investments that allow us to grow our existing wealth.

# Additional Information

A few resources that will help you get up to speed with how to diversify and find new areas for your business to grow in are:

- https://www.inc.com/visa/8-strategies-to-diversify-your-business.html
- https://www.forbes.com/sites/alisoncoleman/2017/04/23/a-diversity-of-ways-to-diversify-your-business/
- https://www.americanexpress.com/us/small-business/openforum/articles/smart-steps-to-diversifying-your-business/
- https://www.entrepreneur.com/article/232881
- https://quickbooks.intuit.com/ca/resources/growing-business/4-ways-to-diversify-your-business-offerings/
- https://www.abcsupply.com/blog/diversify-your-business-in-four-steps

# 14 BALANCING EVERYTHING
## Keeping it all together

To be able to build a successful business, you will have to find the right balance between the amount of time you give to the business and the time you give to yourself. An all work story will harm your business. It is an old saying that business owners tend to be workaholics. They believe that working hard is the route to success. And so, it is – up to a point. This chapter touches upon another of the soft skills needed to win in the cut-throat marketplace of today. It also emphasis on how you can reduce things from getting out of hand by delegation and by keeping a handy timetable for oneself.

The truth of the matter is that overwork can lead to health problem. Excessive stress can lead to lack of fitness, high blood pressure, heart problems, and other health issues. It stifles creativity and kills motivation. A good work-life balance is essential if people are to perform to the best of their abilities.

*Figure 58:Time and money: a precarious balance*

Detailed in this chapter, are procedures on how you can strike a balance in achieving business and life success. Steps outlined here will help you get the most out of both your employees and you with good control over stress and other issues.

## A scientific approach is needed

Qualitative research in psychology has enlightened us in the mechanisms that lead to the functionality of the brain. To help get a work balance, these scientific lessons are of outmost importance.

## Allow the spontaneous flow of creativity

The imaginative pieces of the human mind frequently work enthusiastically when our thought is somewhere else – particularly when we are loose or tired. That is the reason smart thoughts frequently 'fly into our psyches' for the time being. The most ideal approach to tackle an issue imaginatively is to focus on it for some time, at that point forget about it and ease yourself. You can also sleep over a problem to let the creative process resolve its conflicts and get you to the best option given your current limitations.

What times work for you?Some people work better in the first part of the day, others at night. you can do just little to change this – you can adjust to it. try and reflect upon yourself and raise questions as to whom you are and spare the most testing work for the hour of the day when you are at your psychological pinnacle. You can get time to yourself either before the people walk into the office or after everyone has left in the evening. Try keeping some time to yourself to give you the problem-solving edge.

*Figure 59: Planning your day can help you stay sane*

# Keep your schedule reasonable

The evening rundown, ordinarily between 2 pm and 4 pm, is a terrible time to accomplish very intellectual tasks. That is true whether or not you're a morning person or an evening person. Shockingly, taking a rest or 'force rest' at work probably will not send the correct message to your workers. Utilize this period to get straightforward administrator work finished.

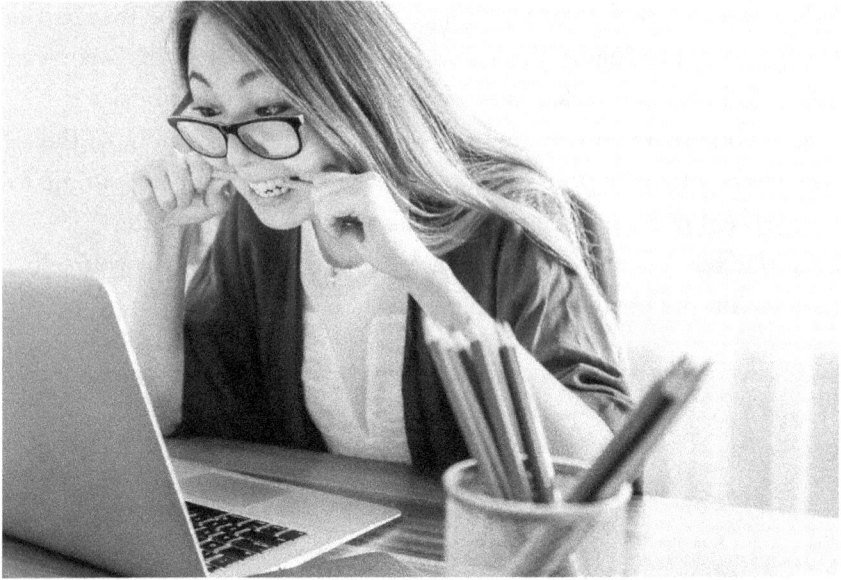

*Figure 60: Stress in moderation is a good thing-- but too much of it is unhealthy.*

## Stress is Acceptable – With Restraint

There's proof that limited quantities of stress every once in a while, may enable our bodies to remain in top condition. Be that as it may, long haul pressure is terrible for us, debilitating our safe mental state and rashly maturing our bodies. In case you are forever worried by your work, the cortisol and adrenaline in your circulatory system from the 'fight or flight reaction' is harming your wellbeing. Time to dial down.

## Find Frameworks that work for you

Hard work and dedication are not avoidable in the pursuit of business success. It is all part of the process!

Be that as it may, it does not in tell that you need to constantly stress yourself by working hard too much. Find a rhythm and get as much done in this phase as possible then give yourself a break. Relax and rebuild your energy levels.

Time will come when your business will demand you to invest in additional energy and extra effort. This may happen when pitching for new customers and clients, applying for funding, or opening another store. It might also happen when new competition is eating away at your business or there is a legal environment change.
Note when you have been working extra hard and when you haven't been. For instance, following three weeks of hard extraordinary work, you may take a weekend off to energize your body and psyche.

Think about your work design as resembling a bank. You 'pay' in unwinding time so you can 'spend' with difficult work when you must. We are not trying to say that you should relax most of the time and let a crisis take shape, it is always better to intervene at the right time and reduce stress for everyone.

# 5 Simple notes for keeping your work-life balance

It is one thing to mean well about your work-life balance, however, here are a few guides to begin with: Learn to distribute tasks
The best business administrators are the individuals who can designate the correct work to the ideal individuals – and afterward, let them continue ahead with it. In case you are a micromanager or somebody who thinks that it is difficult to assign work, attempt to change. Your business is bound to prosper in the event that you gain proficiency with this skill, and you'll feel better as well.

## Take the days you know you need off actually off

If you know that you are going to be going to a family event on a holiday, make sure you are not scheduled to work. Furthermore, make sure that you completely disconnect from work and try to not check emails, work on anything, and just recharge. Furthermore, urge your staff to do likewise. Without a vacation, life can begin to want to be on a treadmill. That is no real way to maintain a business. Take breaks when you can, and benefit as much as possible from your time away from work.

## Keep your health obligations in order

Get standard medical checkups. It will aid in demonstrating whether you have to lessen your outstanding task at hand. Blowing off the people who could tell you the warning signs of overworking, probably isn't the best idea and making sure that you see your doctor can help you keep your personal health in tip top shape.

## Stay medically fit

Eat reasonably, maintain a strategic distance from stressors, ensure that you exercise consistently and get a lot of rest. Keeping your body at balance will enable your brain to adapt to the weights of maintaining your business.

## Switch off

Figure out how to turn yourself off from work appropriately toward the day's end and at ends of the week as well. Fight the temptation to browse your business email or sign into your work frameworks out of hours. Unwind and change jobless mode totally.

*Figure 61: Reorganizing your desk can help you regain a centered mindset.*

# Enhance the working environment

It might not be possible to avoid work; however, you can make your working experience a wonderful. Take a look at these tips:

## Redesign your office

Beanbags, break-out regions, and pool tables function admirably for tech new companies. However, only a couple of basic improvements can improve your workplace. In some cases, a new layer of paint, a couple of plants, and revamping the furniture are everything necessary to light up your workspace and detract from the fact it is just an office.

## Mobilize your Office

**Online based computing implies you do not need to be in the workplace to be online. Regardless of whether its email, bookkeeping programming, inventory management, or conferencing devices, you**

**can take it with you. Online applications can allow you to manage your financial balance and accounts in a cafe, send invoices and receive emails from anywhere. You can have a difference in scene and still complete your work Use natural light to your advantage**

This is significant for your emotional well-being and sleeping patterns. It is regular for some individuals to find it difficult to sleep unless they get a certain amount of daylight. So, if your office, cube, or workspace lacks windows, get out during lunch break, and enjoy natural daylight.

## Try to socialize

Shut entryways and work areas make it harder to associate and interact with your employees, and for them to connect with one another. The best future-focused organizations have workplaces that are explicitly intended to urge individuals to meet, visit and share ideas and thoughts. This improves prosperity and profitability. Hence, urge your staffs and employees to blend and socialize with each other.

## Keep in mind why you are doing business

Recall when you began your business and wonder why you did it. Maybe it was so you could have more autonomy, more cash, you were sick of the monotony, or additional extra time to be with your family. Possibly it was any or even all of those things.

Keep the bigger picture in mind, record them and have them in a spot where you can without much of a stretch see and make reference to them. This will make it simpler to dodge work turning into an end in itself. It is imperative to keep a feeling of that bigger picture. It gives you the motivation to continue. As the well-known adage goes, no one kicked the bucket wishing they'd invested more energy at work.

Your work-life balance influences how good you'll be at maintaining your business. Wasting time ceaselessly will negatively affect both your business and your own life. Take your time to strike a balance and get it right so as to be successful in business and for you to have good health so as to enjoy it. – And the wellbeing and opportunity to appreciate it.

## The Quarterly Plan

One good way to keep a track of the things that should keep you occupied and what should be delegated is to make a quarterly plan. This plan was developed by David Finkel over at INC.com but very applicable to what we are doing.

As a leader of your company, you know it is your job to keep your team and the company focused on the right things. In fact, to successfully scale, you must balance the need to focus on those fewer, better things that will make a leveraged difference for your company and you need to be flexible so you can adjust as you go. It's as if you have a two-sided equation, with your need for flexibility on one side--markets change, opportunities appear, and tactics succeed or fail--and, on the other side, you need to gain momentum and for your staff to have the time to get meaningful blocks of work done.

Essentially, your action plan must be adaptable to the changing circumstances of your marketplace but also heed the high cost of lost momentum and a frustrated team if you change your company's focus too frequently.

So, what is the key to maintaining a dynamic balance between flexibility and momentum? It is the quarter. The quarter is the perfect unit of time to bridge your big-picture goals--which probably have a two-to-five-year timeline or longer--and your weekly planning and daily action. The quarter is the way to execute on your strategy to accomplish your business goals.

It is long enough that you can get meaningful units of work done that collectively bring you closer to your long-term goals, but short enough so that you can frequently course correct and hold your focus.

As per our experience, each business should review their company's quarterly action plan each week. It becomes a clear accountability tool and GPS to ensure your team is focusing on the right things and hitting the key milestones on time. And with your plan being one page, you and your team can take it in with one look.

Here is how to create Your One-Page Quarterly Strategic Action Plan in Three Simple Steps.

## Pick Your Three "Focus Areas" for the Quarter

Your Focus Areas are the most important areas for your business to spotlight during the coming quarter.

Sure, you will still have to take care of your company's day-to-day operational needs. But in your Focus Areas that quarter, you will invest a portion of your best resources, because you know that these are the areas that will really help you scale and develop your business. Each quarter, meet with your leadership team and decide on up to three Focus Areas for your business for that quarter.

Potential Focus Areas could be:

- Increasing your lead flow
- Improving your sales conversion system
- Speeding up your collections cycle
- Making a key hire

- Developing a new product
- Progressing on a key project

I strongly advise you to limit your company to no more than three Focus Areas for the quarter (in many cases, having only one or two Focus Areas for the quarter may be a better choice). Why limit your company to three Focus Areas? Because too many top priorities mean you have no top priorities and it becomes difficult to focus your energies.

Ninety days go fast. If you spread your company too thin, you and your team will partially do things instead of fully doing a few key chunks that actually produce value for your company.
So, pick your Focus Areas carefully and invest your resources to get something special done on these fewer, better areas.

Focus Area 1:

_____

Focus Area 2:

_____

Focus Area 3:

_____

## Clarify the Criteria for Success for Each of Your Three Focus Areas

Now that you have picked your three Focus Areas for the quarter, the temptation is to immediately go lay out your action steps for them.
Do not. Step two requires you to pause first and clarify your success criteria for each.

What would you need to accomplish this quarter to feel successful in this Focus Area?

Be ruthlessly realistic about what it is possible to accomplish in 90 days.

Generally, it is better you pick criteria of success that you have control over (or, at the very least, you have a great deal of influence over). It is important to look for criteria that are as objectively and quantitatively measurable as possible. When criteria are too subjective, you may reach the end of the quarter without agreeing on whether you succeeded.

Also, it is better that for every Focus Area you pick one "Key Performance Indicator" to track. If you look to this KPI to determine your performance, you will know if your company is on track to succeed in this Focus Area.

Look for three to four definite criteria of success for each Focus Area.

Your written criteria of success for each Focus Area give you a yardstick against which to measure progress as you go. Also, by laying out your criteria of success for each Focus Area, you will have clear clues for what action steps you will need to take over the quarter-- most of your action steps will be obvious.

Focus Area 1 Criteria:

_____

_____

_____

_____

Key Indicator:

_____

Focus Area 2 Criteria:

_____

_____

_____

_____

Key Indicator:

_____

Focus Area 3 Criteria:

_____

_____

_____

_____

Key Indicator:

_____

## Lay Out Your Key Action Steps and Milestones for the Quarter

The final step is to lay out the key action steps you need to take and milestones you need to reach to accomplish your criteria of success for each Focus Area over the coming quarter.

To keep your plan to one page, you will probably need to break down each Focus Area into five to seven action steps and milestones.

While your plan must be detailed enough to guide your actions, it must not be so detailed that you feel overwhelmed or lose yourself in the minutia.

For each action step, pick a team member to be ultimately responsible for executing the step by a definite date. While you can have multiple people contribute to a specific step or steps, you need to pick one person who is tasked with the responsibility and authority to get that step done and done well. We say that this person "owns" the task. This sense of ownership is critical to your success. It is hard to hold someone accountable for a missed milestone if it is not clear who was responsible.

With this structure, the owner does not have to do all of the work themselves; they just need to be responsible for making sure that it gets done in the best way possible.

A good way to make these actions happen is by creating quantifiable action steps to plot the path to completion.

Action Steps:

1. _____
2. _____
3. _____
4. _____
5. _____
6. _____
7. _____
8. _____
9. _____
10. _____

Milestones:

_____

_____

_____

_____

_____

_____

_____

_____

_____

_____

_____

_____

_____

## Additional Information

You can explore more on the above from the following sites:

- https://www.xero.com/us/resources/small-business-guides/business-management/work-life-balance/
- https://articles.bplans.com/8-tips-for-entrepreneurs-who-are-balancing-their-business-with-their-day-job/
- https://www.entrepreneur.com/article/277520
- https://www.entrepreneur.com/article/250382
- https://www.inc.com/david-finkel/creating-a-1-page-quarterly-action-plan-for-your-business.html
- http://smallbusiness.chron.com/write-business-action-plan-2750.html

# 15 FURTHERMORE
A look back on where we have been

We have spent the last 14 chapters discussing various aspects of building a business. The truth is that a business, online or not, requires some basics which have not changed over time. The advent of online commerce has only given a flip to how you reach out to customers and how customers connect with the business. Building a business involves both hard skills and a lot of soft skills, ability to understand markets, and an ability to understand people. A lot goes into being a business leader, and this is one aspect that is becoming more complex by the day.

After identifying the niche that one fits into, one still has to work tirelessly to build every aspect from scratch. The flip side is that all this has a big chance of not reaching the intended goal. Statistics tell us that only one in five start-ups last over three years. This should not dishearten you, the ones that do not make it past three years either pivot or find a new niche.

Let us still recapitulate what we have talked about in the book and even try to link it with our hypothetical 3D printing business one last time. The book covers the start and building of a business through 14 chapters as follows:

*Figure 62: Here we are, you did it!*

## Determining the skills you have

This is where we talked about identifying that core skill around which the product/service will be built. One has to understand what really matters to them, they have to dig deep for the answers which will make him commit all his time and energies to build the business.

For 3D printed parts the skill may well be around programming and managing a 3D printer. Many applications of 3D printing are today helping create resolutions that fit every customer's needs. One such example is a custom-made birthday gift. When correctly 3D printed, it is a treasured keepsake for anyone.

## Ideating and honing your skills

The focus now shifts to adding skills that will be needed to run a business successfully. Many soft and hard skills have to be added to one's repertoire before we can be confident of starting a business. This includes the ability to read the market, develop action plans for what to prioritize and how to approach a problem. Additionally, the ability to understand audiences and how the web presence of these audiences can be utilized to build a dedicated customer base is essential to success. How to brainstorm and find answers to difficult business questions is very important as well. Who should be on the forum that advises you on the way forward?

Our business of 3D printed applications would require that we learn and understand the needs of businesses we would do business with as well as the end users. Understand that the audience includes the complete delivery chain and the end consumer for whom we are customizing. We will need to understand how to get inputs for the product needed and the right manufacturing of the component. We will require a fair knowledge of the e-commerce environment to be able to establish the business and find solutions to problems we may face in establishing the business.

## Researching your market

Once we have validated the basic idea and gained the added advantage of modifying the concepts with feedback from potential customers, we are ready for some market research. This will cover many aspects including competition, pricing, point of sale, marketing requirements, where our audience socializes on the net, The best distributors, and things like this. The ability to research well will save a lot of work later. It will give you insights to make finer changes to the business plan and the product or service so that it is better accepted in the market.

For the 3D printed parts business, we have to be extremely sensitive to the voice of the customer. We must build robust listening processes so that the right feedback reaches us on time. All future business decisions will be based on the quality of research we can do in and around our market.

# Validating your idea

Once the core idea is finalized and we are ready with our machine for the next move, we must spend time validating the idea we are working on. It is better to try and find a market now than invest all the time and resources in building a product or service and realize that there is no customer or that the market is so saturated that we will not be able to make money even with a superior product or service.

This is the time to build feedback groups, or a list of trusted advisors. An early feedback group, a list for test marketing, and a proof of concept product or service which we can pitch to our target audience and analyze the response will allow us to test our idea in controlled conditions. This will help you also understand the price people will pay for the product or service and tweak our project as per the feedback received.

These topics are a lot of groundwork that we have to do for any business, not really customized for a specific one as the 3D printing business we have been talking about throughout the book. Building an advisor list here will be a bit complicated as we need to reach out to a number of different stakeholders. From people in the 3D printing field to potential customers and even large custom business owners. Building a good list of early adopters will be a good challenge when approaching the validation stage of our 3D printed parts business.

## Talking to customers

Business exit to fulfil a gap in the market. This gap is defined best buy the customers. The business will exist till the time there is a need for the goods and services it produces. A market is a dynamic place where customer preferences change every day. By talking to customers, we ensure that we are in line with the requirements and that we will launch a product/service needed by the customers. If we find any misalignment in all this, then corrective steps are taken. These steps are often called a pivot and would help course correct a business.

This is a critical step and a continuous requirement for any business. An ear to what the customer is saying is crucial to long-term success. This is a soft skill which is the cornerstone of the strategies which will bring success to the venture. Our 3D printing business is a bit complex and it would be good to identify the various audiences we call as customers and build a mechanism to listen to them regularly and to analyze the input for business course correction.

## Building your money-making machine

We are trying to establish the required ingredients to launch an internet-based business. One key component in doing this will be the computer that is central to our business. Understanding the demands that the business will have on the machine is critical to be able to build/obtain a machine which will support us over a period of time. More often than not this requires that we build a machine as per our requirements as against buying off the shelf. This approach is not only more flexible but also cost-effective. We need to understand what goes into a good machine and where to get components and other help for putting together a good machine. This section also talks about the need for website hosting and other aspects of building the IT infrastructure that will help launch a web-based business.

The business we are trying to use as a test case (3D component printing) is completely dependent on the web for its outreach. We will require building a machine that not only does the order and inventory management but also can run the 3D printer that the business runs on. This is also a place where Fitzgerald Tech Solutions will be able to support your quest to get the right things in place from the start.

## Getting the wheels rolling

With the basics in place and with a good amount of market study done it is now time to start putting all the documentation in place. Launching a business is a complex activity which will require an understanding of what the business wants, what the funding agencies want and what the law dictates. Some important documents we need are:

- Privacy Policy
- Terms of Service
- Shareholder Agreement
- Articles of Incorporation
- Contract for work, or Statement of Work
- Outside Contractor Agreement
- Non-Disclosure Agreement
- Intellectual Property Protection

This is about being organized and being legally compliant. It is essential and is required by the law of the land. Should not be overlooked as it can lead to a lot of legal issues as well. This is not about any specific type of business and is an integral part of any business. We do advise getting a good corporate law firm to help put all the legal part of the business in place, just as our 3d parts business will be utilizing to get the correct documents in place

## Making your idea a reality

It is now time to put all things together and prepare to make the business a reality. This will require that we put some suppliers and partners in place. We would have to decide where will we manufacture or procure our products from. Finalizing a supplier has many aspects including cost, time, quality, and quantity that must be balanced. Once the supplier part is in place, we will require a partner to create and maintain our digital assets like the website and the social media accounts.

Every business will have to do this, this is irrespective of the line of work or industry, especially in today's day and age. The really good part is that we at Fitzgerald Tech Solutions can be of great help in building and maintaining your digital assets. Reach out to us and we can partner in a fruitful journey of growth for each other. With our 3d printed parts business, we will be able to purchase the materials for the machine, create the website and get ready for the launch of our business.

## To the moon – the business launch

It is now time to take our business to its logical start. It is time to launch for customers to start paying us for the goods and services offered. Given that this is an e-commerce business we have to find answers to a number of teething issues including how to realize payments and how to manage orders and inventory online. We will have to build customer engagement models and also create the right noise for the launch. We will have to find ways to reach as many potential customers as we can without burning a hole in our pockets.

This is an activity which is required for all businesses and would have some customization depending on the area of business. With a solution used by people on Facebook, our audience is well defined and thus easy to reach. This reduces cost and time required to make people aware of what we bring to the table.

## Keeping yourself alive – continued involvement

Building and launching is done! It is now time to shift focus on running the day to day business. This will require that we attract new customers regularly and maintain a healthy engagement with the existing ones. This also requires us to stay competitive so that our customers are not taken away by competition. We will have to build blogs and enlarge our e-mail marketing efforts; we will have to engage better with the target audience and try to become an active contributor to our society.

For the 3D printing business, this would entail launching an authoritative blog that guides customers on the benefits of using custom built 3D printed components to reduce the cost of manufacturing and for creative customized gifts. It also involves adopting new tech to ensure we deliver best results for the consumer. We may also engage with the larger community by writing for their publications or calling them to contribute to our blog.

## Marketing yourself and your idea

This is an area of specialization today, just so much to talk about and do that we simply cannot cover everything in a single go. To put things in place, we must understand how search engines rank pages and try to be compliant with them to feature on the first page of the search engine results. We should also make intelligent investments into SEM and ensure that the right keywords are identified and bought to attract the customers. We should also be members of the right forums on social media platforms and if required we should invest in advertising on them. Working with affiliates can increase our reach and give rich returns in terms of new customers.

Every business needs a proper marketing plan, the right investment in the vehicles that will take our message to the target audience. Designing the message is in itself an art. If you find yourself a little lost in all this, it is fine to engage an agency to do the heavy lifting for you. Just be sure of defining clear measurable goals which you can monitor along with the agency to ensure things are on track.

Utilizing the proper social media marketing for our 3d printed parts business will be essential as we continue to run the business and generate sales. Targeting, refining, and pivoting marketing campaigns to the ones that generate leads here is essential.

## Growth

Business needs continuous attention and a drive for growth. If there is stagnation, there is a tendency for customers to move to new businesses and a fear of losing the market we have so painstakingly created. Growth can be achieved in multiple ways, new products, new markets, new customer segments but what is fundamental is that growth comes with higher sales and adding more customers or billing more from the same customer. This requires the business owner to spend a disproportionate amount of time in the sales or customer-facing functions. This will require you to hire new team members and start delegating more so that you still have time for running sales effectively.

For our 3D printing business, we can well increase our product line from custom parts built for engineers or consumers to parts for non-manufactured or obsolete items for repair. All this will help attract more customers, we can also engage with more hospitals and clinics to grow our business. The core will still be the ability of the business owner to guide and engage with a greater number of potential customers.

# Diversifying your portfolio

Once you are satisfied with the pace of business growth it is time to start thinking about diversification. This is where the entire process of identifying a skill and matching it with the market gap starts again. It is like launching a new business all over again. You already know how taxing this can be but having done so once we now know that we have the ability to do it again. This may also be the biggest growth driver your business needed. One has to be careful of not losing control of the running business while pushing for diversification.

The 3D printing business we have talked about has focused only on trinkets and gifts, as well as small parts. It may well be time to start doing 3D printing for the industry as a whole or potentially medical prosthetics. A 3D printing solution can remarkably reduce time to market for new products. It can reduce the cost of casting and make otherwise costly products available to masses. There is a lot of new applications getting acceptance every day and we must carve our niche in all of this. The skill upgrade required may be substantial, but the investment is bound to bring in rich dividends in the form of new business.

# Balancing everything

Lastly, we must always remember that we are building all this for a more rewarding life. Nothing is greater than the quality of life we lead, and the work should not generate so much stress that we are unable to enjoy the small things in life. Take that long-awaited break, enjoy time with family and friends, go to the town fair or the evening theatre. Spend time at the cinemas or just relax at home, always remember that the business will only grow if we take good care of it by first taking good care of our self.

## Conclusion

With that, this book is brought to a close. We have taken you through all it takes to start an online business and hopefully you now have the skills, research, drive, and motivation to get it done! Go out there and make it happen! Anyone can change the world. I wish you a rewarding and enriching entrepreneurial journey!

# ABOUT THE AUTHOR

Matthew J Fitzgerald was born in Mount Prospect, Illinois, and has spent his entire life living there. From an early age, he was entrepreneurially inclined. In third grade, he learned the entire entrepreneurial concept of selling things for more than you paid for them. He bought a machine that allowed you to melt old crayons down and make new ones, and from there, he would sell the customized and funky looking crayons to his peers for a profit. He would charge a quarter a crayon and make a considerable profit from the broken and discarded crayons that the school was getting rid of.

Additionally, he also started to learn a lot about technology and picking up programming and information technology best habits from the myriad of books that he would read on the subjects. He also had the thought that he should have a notebook where he should document the many ideas he had. He started an idea notebook around this time, and from the more whimsical ideas of a child to the more solid ideas of an adult, all of his ideas are well documented and able to be referenced.

From there, he attended high school and was further pushed in an entrepreneurial sense. He was asked by the staff of his high school, because they saw that he knew a lot about technology, to build them a school store website. This would be the place where they would sell all the school's merchandise online. There was a twist, though, He would also design the spirit wear for the whole school. Fitzgerald and his friend Matt worked on the entire process and made about ten designs that were sold to the school. In addition, he made the entire site and designed it to match the school's colors and main theme.

After he got that project finished, he was asked to help make a site for the school to distribute the news services and consult on redesigning the school's landing page. Then he noticed a reoccurring theme: Everyone wanted him to make websites for them, but he was doing a large amount of work pro bono, not making any money. After he noticed that phenomenon, he developed the idea for Fitzgerald Tech Solutions, a web hosting, and web design company that would be able to satisfy the needs of people who had been approaching him to build websites as well as making a decent amount of money on the side. As he approached college, he worked to try and further tune this business model and launch it. As he got accepted into Purdue in Systems Design, and eventually, the Entrepreneurship and Innovation learning community, he noticed that this model had potential. After completing entrepreneurship classes, he felt like he was ready to launch, so he did. Since then, the business has been growing at an astounding rate, and he has been approached by more people to do more diverse technical work that requires very high technical skills.

To reorganize his ventures and plan for future intellectual properties and other businesses, he created MJF Ventures, LLC, to act as the holding company for all of his future ventures.

Some of the pivotal influencers in his life have been his parents, who have supported his somewhat odd and creative habits as a child and have given him what he would consider a good head on his shoulders. Additionally, they are helping him attain my goals by helping to finance his private education for as long as he has been alive, and they also allowed him to take over a room in the house to house all of my servers, technical junk, and drum set. He will forever be grateful for their astounding generosity, support, and love for him. Additionally, a few of his mentors have played a pivotal part in the creation of Fitzgerald Tech Solutions in its current form, as well as his friends.

Today, he still operates Fitzgerald Tech Solutions and has helped start numerous other online ventures for his clients.

# APPENDIX 1: LIST OF FIGURES

# APPENDIX 2: LIST OF BUSINESS IDEAS

1. Web hosting
2. graphic design
3. Consulting
4. email marketing
5. social media engagement
6. social media marketing
7. Social network
8. blog
9. E-commerce store
10. Nice Revenue blog
11. Business plan services
12. Computer repair
13. remote technical assistance
14. Copy editing
15. proofreading
16. indexing
17. editing
18. Video Editor
19. ghostwriting
20. copywriting
21. Electronics repair
22. event planning
23. Website migration services
24. website monitoring services
25. web developer
26. web designer
27. Remote assistant
28. Used bookseller
29. Computer training purveyor
30. Desktop publisher
31. Photographer
32. videographer
33. Website reviewer
34. Youtuber
35. Freelancer.com
36. Take Surveys
37. App Tester
38. Online tutoring
39. Paid Reviewer
40. Mechanical Turk
41. Data Entry
42. Online Travel
43. Amazon associates
44. Security Consultant
45. Fix Search Engine Errors
46. Online Juror
47. eBay seller
48. Amazon seller
49. Animator

# WORKS CITED

"Adventures In Marketing Your Ecommerce Business.". *Paypal.Com*, 2018, https://www.paypal.com/us/brc/article/adventures-in-marketing-your-online-business. Accessed 15 May 2018.

"Section 5. Developing an Action Plan." *Chapter 8. Developing a Strategic Plan | Section 5. Developing an Action Plan | Main Section | Community Tool Box*, 2020, ctb.ku.edu/en/table-of-contents/structure/strategic-planning/develop-action-plans/main.

"SWOT Analysis: Discover New Opportunities, Manage And Eliminate Threats". *Mindtools.Com*, 2018, https://www.mindtools.com/pages/article/newTMC_05.htm. Accessed 15 May 2018.

"The Top 20 Reasons Startups Fail". *CB Insights Research*, 2018, https://www.cbinsights.com/research/startup-failure-reasons-top/. Accessed 15 May 2018.

"What Are Washington State Business Structures?". *Washington Secretary Of State*, 2018, https://www.sos.wa.gov/corps/registration_structures.aspx. Accessed 15 May 2018.

"What Is 3D Printing? How Does A 3D Printer Work? Learn 3D Printing". *3D Printing*, 2018, https://3Dprinting.com/what-is-3D-printing/. Accessed 15 May 2018.

Barringer, Bruce, and R. Duane Ireland. *Entrepreneurship: Successfully Launching New Ventures Purdue University*. 1st ed., Pearson Learning Solution, 2015.

*Business Planning Timeline*. University Of Wisconsin Milwaukee, 2018, http://www4.uwm.edu/sce/resources/sbdc/BusinessPlanningTimeli ne.pdf. Accessed 15 May 2018.

Chudoba, B. "Validating Your Decisions Using Surveys". *For Entrepreneurs*, 2018, https://www.forentrepreneurs.com/surveys/. Accessed 15 May 2018.

Crider, Michael. "How to Build Your Own Computer, Part One: Choosing Hardware." How, How-To Geek, 11 Dec. 2017, www.howtogeek.com/howto/the-geek-blog/building-a-new-computer-part-1-choosing-hardware/.

Dame, Nate. "The Complete Guide To Optimizing Content For SEO (With Checklist) - Search Engine Land". *Search Engine Land*, 2018, https://searchengineland.com/complete-guide-optimizing-content-seo-checklist-269884. Accessed 15 May 2018.

Demers, Jayson. "Your Guide To Marketing An Online Business". *Inc.Com*, 2018, https://www.inc.com/jayson-demers/your-guide-to-marketing-an-online-business.html. Accessed 15 May 2018.

Finkel, David. "Creating A 1-Page Quarterly Action Plan For Your Business". *Inc.Com*, 2018, https://www.inc.com/david-finkel/creating-a-1-page-quarterly-action-plan-for-your-business.html. Accessed 15 May 2018.

Haden, Jeff. "Start a Business: 9 Steps to Validate a Business Idea While Keeping Your Full Time Job." Inc.com, Inc., 16 Jan. 2017, www.inc.com/jeff-haden/start-a-business-9-steps-to-validate-a-business-idea-while-keeping-your-full-tim.html.

Landau, Candice. "Business Startup Checklist - Bplans Blog". *Bplans Blog*, 2018, https://articles.bplans.com/business-startup-checklist/. Accessed 15 May 2018.

*Marketing Benchmarks From 7000 Businesses*. HubSpot, 2018, http://cdn1.hubspot.com/hub/53/Marketing-Benchmarks-from-7000-businesses.pdf. Accessed 15 May 2018.

Osterwalder, Alexander, Yves Pigneur, Tim Clark, and Alan Smith. *Business Model Generation: A Handbook for Visionaries, Game Changers, and Challengers.* , 2010. Print.

Ries, Eric. The Lean Startup: How Constant Innovation Creates Radically Successful Businesses. Penguin Business, 2019.

RNCOS. "What Is A Marketing Initiative?" Singapore Travel Guide, 2020, www.streetdirectory.com/travel_guide/17636/marketing/what_is_a_marketing_initiative.html.

Robinson, Ryan. "9 Steps To Validate A Business Idea In 30 Days With $500". *How To Start A Profitable Side Business With Ryan Robinson*, 2018, https://www.ryrob.com/validate-business-idea/. Accessed 15 May 2018.

Sugars, Brad. "How to Research Your Market." *Entrepreneur*, 2 Mar. 2007, www.entrepreneur.com/article/175276.

*The Craap Test.* California State University, Chico, 2010, https://www.csuchico.edu/lins/handouts/eval_websites.pdf. Accessed 15 May 2018.

Tobak, Steve. "The True Meaning of 'Entrepreneur'." *Entrepreneur*, 3 Apr. 2015, www.entrepreneur.com/article/244565

Washington State Department of Revenue. "Choose an Ownership Structure." Choose an Ownership Structure | Washington Department of Revenue, Washington State, 2019, bls.dor.wa.gov/ownershipstructures.aspx.

Www.shoppingcartelite.com.au. "HOW TO FIND A MANUFACTURER OR SUPPLIER FOR YOUR PRODUCT IDEA." Shopping Cart Elite, 2020, www.shoppingcartelite.com/articles/how-to-find-a-manufacturer-or-supplier.

Xtensio. "How To: Create a Business Model Canvas." Xtensio, 18 Apr. 2020, xtensio.com/how-to-create-a-business-model-canvas/.

Yang, James. "Four Types of Intellectual Property to Protect Your Idea and How to Use Them Patent Attorney - Orange County - OC Patent Lawyer." Patent Attorney | Orange County | OC Patent Lawyer, 18 Mar. 2020, ocpatentlawyer.com/four-types-intellectual-property-protect-idea/.

www.ingramcontent.com/pod-product-compliance
Lightning Source LLC
Chambersburg PA
CBHW060541200326
41521CB00007B/438